Science
Olympiad

Highly useful for all school students participating
in various Olympiads & Competitions

Series Editor Keshav Mohan
Author Shahana Ansari

Class 4

arihant
ARIHANT PRAKASHAN, MEERUT

ARIHANT PRAKASHAN, MEERUT

All Rights Reserved

ꢸ **Administrative & Production Offices**

Corporate Office 'Ramchhaya' 4577/15, Agarwal Road, Darya Ganj New Delhi -110002
Tele: 011- 47630600, 43518550; Fax: 011- 23280316

Head Office Kalindi, TP Nagar, Meerut (UP) - 250002
Tele: 0121-2401479, 2512970, 4004199; Fax: 0121-2401648

All disputes subject to Meerut (UP) jurisdiction only.

ꢸ **Sales & Support Offices**

Agra, Ahmedabad, Bengaluru, Bhubaneswar, Bareilly, Chennai, Delhi, Guwahati, Haldwani, Hyderabad, Jaipur, Jalandhar, Jhansi, Kolkata, Kota, Lucknow, Meerut, Nagpur & Pune

ꢸ **ISBN** 978-93-5251-203-4

ꢸ **Price** ₹65

Typeset by Arihant DTP Unit at Meerut
Printed & Bound by Arihant Publications (I) Ltd. (Press Unit)

Production Team

Publishing Manager	Mahendra Singh Rawat	Page Layouting	Krishna Kumar Saini
Project Head	Mona Yadav	DTP Operator	Manoj Garg, Shishpal
Project Coordinator	Shahid Saifi	Cover Designer	Syed Darin Zaidi
Proof Reader	Mamta Sharma	Inner Designer	Deepak Kumar

For further information about the products from Arihant
log on to www.arihantbooks.com or email to info@arihantbooks.com

Preface

Science Olympiad Series for Class 2nd-10th is a series of books which will challenge the young inquisitive minds by the non-routine and exciting problems based on concept of Science.

The main purpose of this series is to make the students ready for competitive exams. The school/board exams are of qualifying nature but not competitive, they do not help the students to prepare for competitive exams, which mainly have objective questions.

Need of Olympiad Series
This series will fill this gap between the School/Board and Competitive exams as this series have all questions in objective format. This series helps students who are willing to sharpen their problem solving skills. Unlike typical assessment books, which emphasis on drilling practice, the focus of this series is on practicing problem solving techniques.

Development of Logical Approach
The thought provoking questions given in this series will help students to attain a deeper understanding of the concepts and through which students will be able to impart Reasoning/Logical/Analytical skills in themselves.

Complement Your School Studies
This series complements the additional preparation needs of students for regular school/board exams. Along with, it will also address all the requirements of the students who are approaching National/State level Olympiads.

I shall welcome criticism from the students, teachers, educators and parents. I would also like to hear from all of you about errors and deficiencies, which may have remained in this edition and the suggestions for the next edition.

Editor

Contents

1. Matter 1-6
2. Animals 7-11
3. Plants 12-16
4. Livings, Transportation and Communication 17-21
5. Our Body 22-26
6. Food 27-30
7. Our Universe 31-34
8. Water 35-39
9. Work, Force and Energy 40-44
10. Our Environment 45-48

Practice Sets **49-52**
Answers and Explanations **53-76**

Matter

1. Which of the following are not matter?

A. Shadow

B. Rain

C. Heat from Sun

D. Cloud

Choose the correct option.

(a) *A* and *B*   (b) *B* and *D*   (c) *A* and *C*   (d) *C* and *D*

2. Table given below shows the properties of three states of matter *A, B* and *C*.

Matter	Definite shape	Definite volume	Can be compressed
A	No	Yes	No
B	No	No	Yes
C	Yes	Yes	No

Which of the following options gives the correct states of *A, B* and *C*?

	A	*B*	*C*
(a)	Gas	Solid	Liquid
(b)	Liquid	Gas	Solid
(c)	Gas	Liquid	Solid
(d)	Liquid	Solid	Gas

3. Choose the correct option which represents the property and state of a material most appropriately.

	Material	Property	State
(a)	Milk	Definite volume	Gas
(b)	Shampoo	Definite shape	Liquid
(c)	Oxygen	Definite size	Gas
(d)	Salt	Definite shape	Solid

4. Observe the figure given below carefully that depicts a piece of clay before and after it was reshaped.

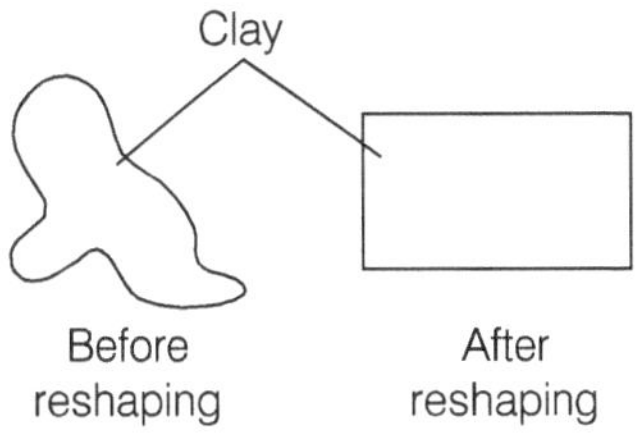

What changes has taken place when the clay was reshaped?

  I. Mass has changed.

  II. Shape has changed.

  III. Volume has changed.

Choose the correct option.

(a) Only I

(b) Only II

(c) I and III

(d) II and III

5. Consider the classification of matter and non-matter given below and choose the correct one.

	Matter	Non-matter
(a)	Ice, air, heat	Oil, cream, thunder
(b)	Fish, paper, sound	Water, plastic, dust
(c)	Fire, butter, air	Wind, wax, light
(d)	Snow, toothbrush, dust	Light, heat, sound

Direction (Q. No. 6) *Study the classification given below carefully and answer the questions that follow:*

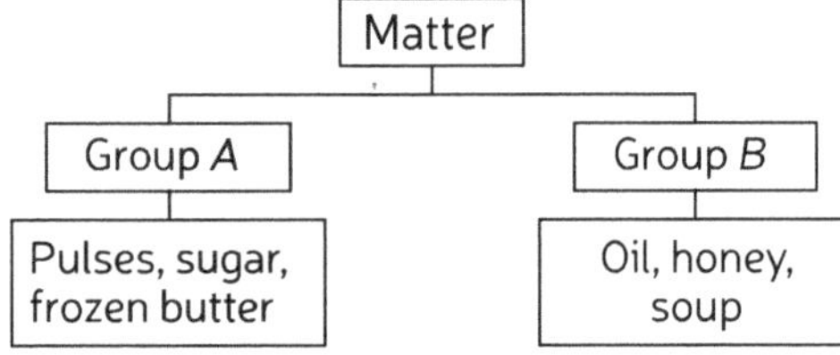

6. What is the similarity between objects in group A and objects in group B?

   I. They all are matter.

   II. They cannot be compressed.

   III. They have definite volume.

   IV. They have mass.

Choose the correct option.
(a) I and II
(b) I, III and IV
(c) I and IV
(d) All of the above

7. Two identical air filled balloons A and B were placed on each end of a rod of a weighing balance which is as shown below. Accidently, balloon B got punchured and air escaped out. The whole set-up is shown below:

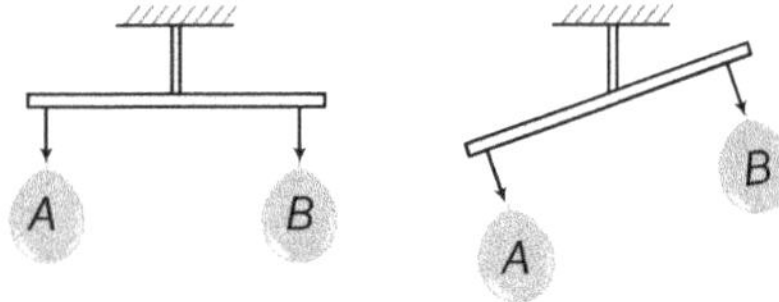

The above experiment confirms that
(a) gases have definite volume
(b) gases have no definite volume
(c) gases cannot be compressed
(d) gases have mass

8. In order to get the most suitable material to make a raincoat, Vishal conducted some tests on materials A, B, C and D.

The results are shown in table below:

Property	A	B	C	D
Flexible	No	Yes	No	Yes
Waterproof	Yes	Yes	Yes	No
Breaks when dropped	Yes	No	No	No

Which of the following materials should he use?
(a) A   (b) B   (c) C   (d) D

9. Observe the set-up arranged by Shobhit shown below carefully. He placed a beaker on a wooden wedge containing two substances P and Q. Then, he removed the wedge and left the beaker on table.

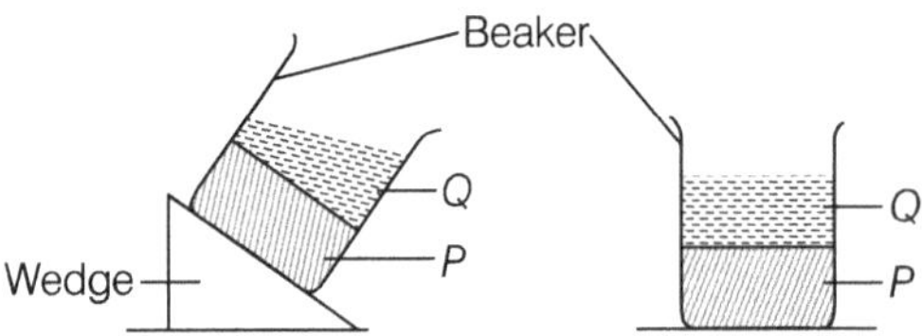

What is the state of substances P and Q?

	P	Q
(a)	Solid	Liquid
(b)	Solid	Gas
(c)	Liquid	Solid
(d)	Liquid	Gas

10. Four kids A, B, C and D observed three bags containing rice, sand and coins in each as shown below:

They made the following comments as listed below:

   I. All three bags have different mass.

   II. All three bags have same mass.

   III. Substances of three bags have different volume.

Science Olympiad Class IV

IV. Substances of three bags have same volume.

Which of them made the correct observation?

(a) I and III   (b) II and III   (c) I and IV   (d) II and IV

11. Daniel half-filled a syringe with water such that it contained equal volume of both water and air. He then placed his finger at the open end of the syringe as shown in the figure below:

Which of the following change will be observed, when the plunger of syringe is push in?

	Volume of water	Volume of air
(a)	Does not change	Does not change
(b)	Increases	Decreases
(c)	Does not change	Decreases
(d)	Decreases	Does not change

12. Observe the classification of matter as shown below carefully:

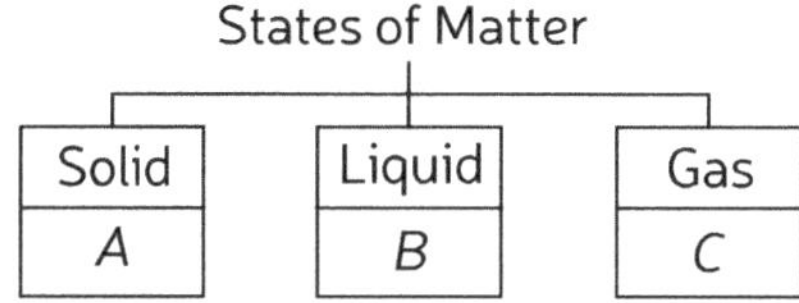

States of Matter

Solid	Liquid	Gas
A	B	C

In which of the boxes snow flakes belong?

(a) Only A   (b) Only B   (c) A and C   (d) B and C

Direction (Q. Nos. 13-14) *Observe the classification of substances A, B and C as shown below carefully and answer the questions that follow:*

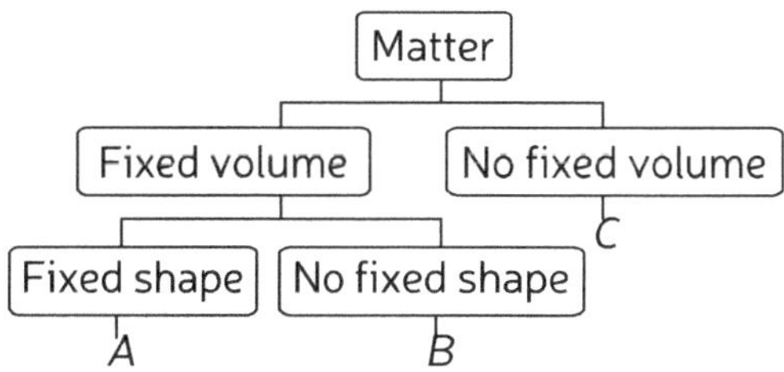

Matter

Fixed volume — No fixed volume
C

Fixed shape — No fixed shape
A   B

13. Which of the substance(s) is (are) compressible in nature?

(a) A   (b) B
(c) C   (d) Both A and B

14. Oil and milk belongs to which types of substances, respectively?

(a) B
(b) B, C
(c) A, C
(d) Either A or C

15. In order to check the hardness of some materials X, Y and Z. Ritu did an experiment. She scratched each material one by one using wooden and plastic rods.

The observations of her experiment are listed below:

Rods used	Scratches observed		
	A	B	C
Plastic	Yes	No	Yes
Wood	No	Yes	Yes

Which of the following statements is correct?

(a) A and B are harder than plastic
(b) B is harder than wood
(c) C is harder than both plastic and wood
(d) B is harder than plastic

16. The flowchart given below shows the properties of certain materials A, B, C and D.

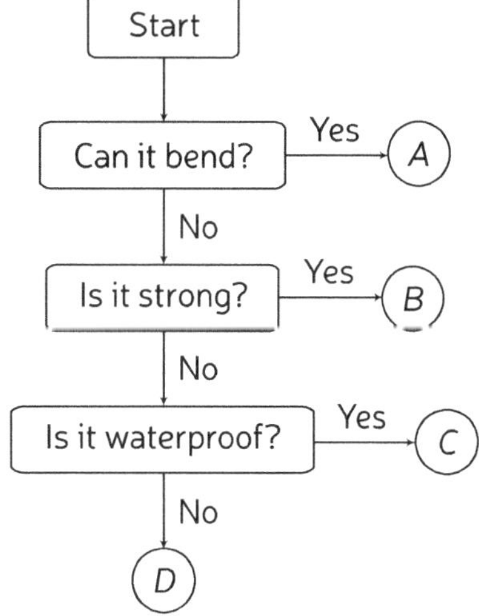

On the basis of the characteristics shown above, which of the following materials can be used to make the book shelf shown in figure below?

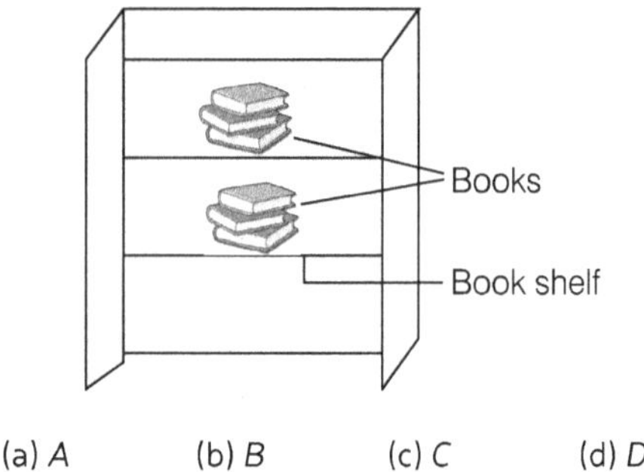

(a) A   (b) B   (c) C   (d) D

17. The diagram shown below depicts a substance P in a tilted cup when kept at room temperature and when heated.

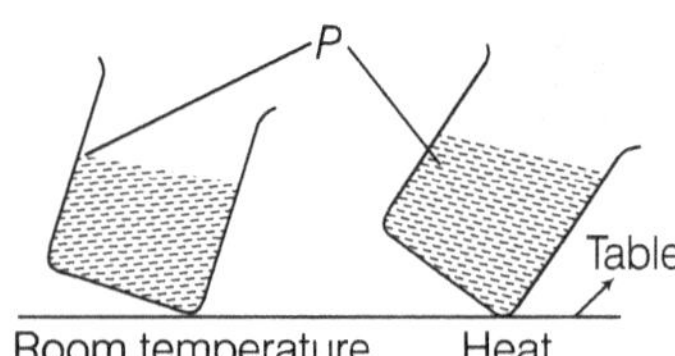

Which of the following best represents substance P when it is heated?

	Possess mass	Fixed shape	Fixed volume
(a)	Yes	Yes	Yes
(b)	No	No	No
(c)	No	Yes	No
(d)	Yes	No	Yes

18. Given below are three cylinders of same size but made of different materials.

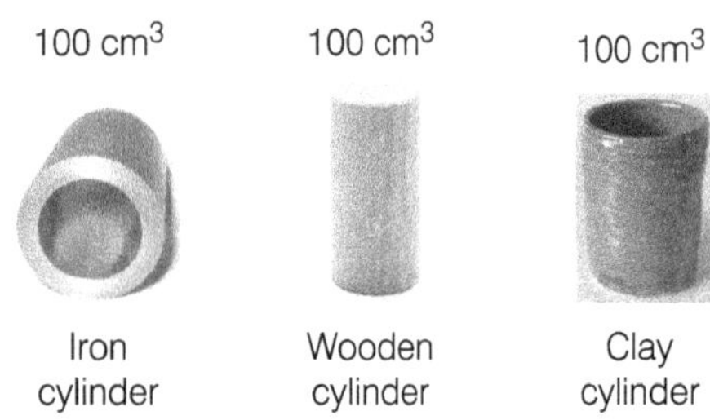

Which of the following statements about the three cylinders is correct?
(a) They all constitutes equal mass
(b) They all have same volume
(c) Only clay and iron cylinder have same mass
(d) Iron cannot be compressed but wooden and clay cylinders can be compressed

19. Four cubes A, B, C and D made up of different substances having same volume are kept on levers shown below in order to compare their masses.

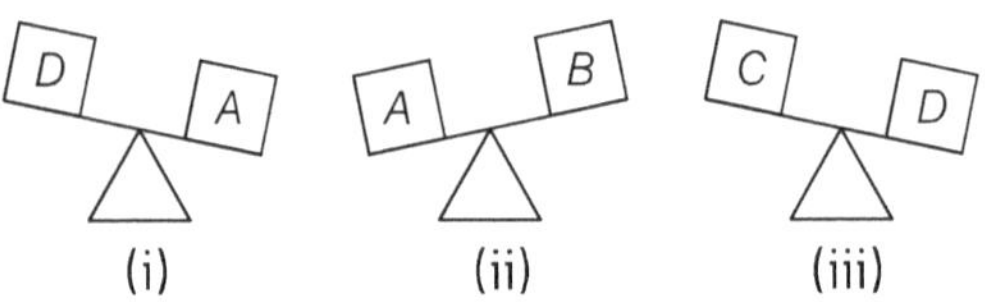

Which of them has highest mass?
(a) A   (b) B
(c) C   (d) D

20. Observe the figure shown below carefully which depicts a cooking pan. The parts of the pan are labelled as X and Y.

Which of the following options best represent the materials being used for X and Y?

	X	Y
(a)	Metal	Metal
(b)	Metal	Wood
(c)	Plastic	Wood
(d)	Plastic	Metal

21. In order to weigh two blocks of same material and same size, Rishabh used two spring balances made up of different materials shown below:

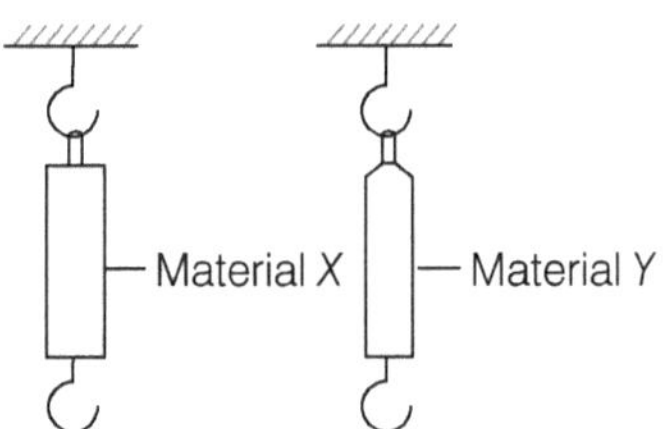

When he hung the blocks, one of the balance broke down as shown below:

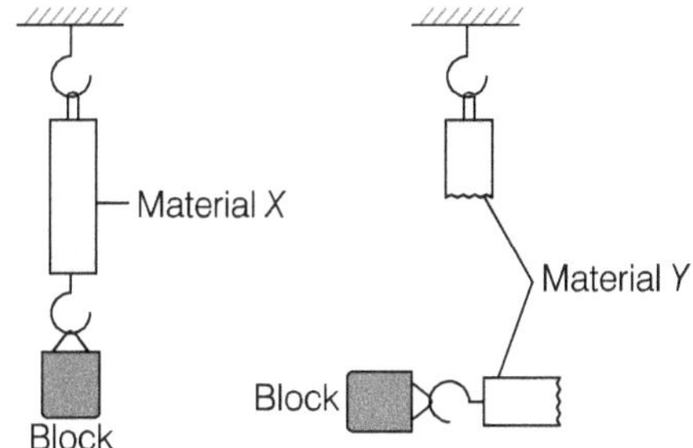

Which of the following statements is true in context with the above observation?
(a) Material *X* is harder than material *Y*
(b) Material *X* is stronger than material *Y*
(c) Material *X* is more elastic than material *Y*
(d) Material *X* is more flexible than material *Y*

22. The diagram below shows two containers of same size balanced on a lever.

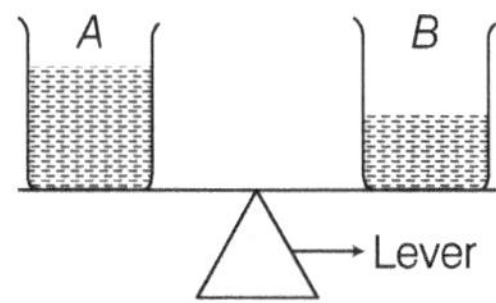

Which of the following statements are true about liquid *A* and liquid *B*?
I. Liquid *A* and liquid *B* have same mass.
II. Liquid *B* has a smaller volume than liquid *A*.
III. Liquid *A* occupies the same amount of space as liquid *B*.
IV. Liquid *A* can be compressed while liquid *B* cannot be compressed.

Choose the correct option.
(a) I and II
(b) II and III
(c) I, II and III
(d) I, II, III and IV

23. Complete the passage using words given in options below:

Everything which exist on ......*A*...... can be grouped into ......*B*...... states of matter. These are solid, ...*C*...... or gas. The general properties that we look in a matter are its ......*D*...... , volume and ......*E*...... .

Codes

	A	*B*	*C*	*D*	*E*
(a)	Ground	three	liquid	shape	mass
(b)	Earth	two	gaseous	size	weight
(c)	Room	four	fluid	shape	weight
(d)	Earth	three	liquid	mass	shape

24. Fill in the blanks using words given in options below:
I. ......*A*...... is the smallest part of matter.
II. The molecules of ......*B*...... are loosely packed compared to solids and tightly packed compared to ......*C*...... .
III. Volume is the amount of ......*D*...... a matter occupies.
IV. Matter has ......*E*...... .

Codes

	A	*B*	*C*	*D*	*E*
(a)	mass	atom	liquid	gas	space
(b)	atom	liquid	gas	space	mass
(c)	space	gas	liquid	mass	space
(d)	gas	liquid	atom	mass	size

25. State true/false using the codes given below:
I. Liquids can be held freely in hand.
II. Solid moth balls directly convert into gas using sublimation.
III. The molecules of a solid are arranged slightly apart from each other.
IV. Solids have definite shape and mass.
V. A molecule is formed when two or more atoms join together.

Codes

	I	II	III	IV	V
(a)	F	F	T	T	T
(b)	T	T	F	F	F
(c)	F	T	F	T	T
(d)	T	F	T	F	F

26. Match the given matrix as per the process involved in the conversion of states:

A. Milk → icecream	(i)	Evaporation
B. Clouds → raindrops	(ii)	Condensation
C. Water vapours → clouds	(iii)	Precipitation
D. Ice → water	(iv)	Melting
	(v)	Freezing

Codes

	A	B	C	D
(a)	(i)	(ii)	(iii)	(iv)
(b)	(iv)	(i)	(ii)	(iii)
(c)	(ii)	(i)	(iv)	(v)
(d)	(v)	(iii)	(ii)	(iv)

Direction (Q. Nos. 27-28) *Read the following information carefully and answer the questions that follow:*

In order to understand the three states of matter, one can think about water. If it freezes into solid, it become ice and atoms are packed together keeping its shape. If it is heated, it will melt into liquid to become water. Slowly, the water will turn into water vapours which is gaseous form of water.

27. Which form of water is solid?

(a) Water
(b) Ice
(c) Water vapours
(d) Water flowing in rivers

28. If you are given water, ice and water vapours enclosed in a container, then how will you recognise the type of matter they are?

(a) Ice flows freely while water and gas has definite shape
(b) Water flows freely while gas and ice has definite shape
(c) Ice possess definite shape while water has only definite volume and water vapours fly away
(d) Either (b) or (c)

29. Solve the following crossword using hints given below:

Across

1. The amount of space occupied by a matter ....

(a) volume   (b) degree   (c) bottom   (d) liquid

3. The tiny particles that join to make up a matter ....

(a) bomb
(b) mass
(c) atom
(d) cell

7. Water in the form of gas is ....

(a) water vapour
(b) vaporisation
(c) evaporation
(d) meteorology

8. Solid white flakes of water that fall from the sky are known as ....

(a) data
(b) laws
(c) snow
(d) test

Down

2. Raindrops are in the state of ....

(a) volume
(b) liquid
(c) circle
(d) matter

4. The amount of matter contained is ....

(a) cell
(b) mass
(c) snow
(d) tube

5. When atoms are in this state, they fly around freely ....

(a) oil
(b) gas
(c) ice
(d) lab

6. The process in which liquid water turns into gas ....

(a) evaporation
(b) temperature
(c) volcanology
(d) water vapour

Animals

1. Match the following animals with the term used for the group of these animals.

A. Elephant   (i) Pride
B. Lions   (ii) Band
C. Monkeys   (iii) School
D. Fish   (iv) Herd

Codes

	A	B	C	D
(a)	(iv)	(i)	(ii)	(iii)
(b)	(iii)	(iv)	(i)	(ii)
(c)	(ii)	(iii)	(iv)	(i)
(d)	(i)	(ii)	(iii)	(iv)

2. What advantage do migratory birds have by flying in 'V' formation?
   (a) This reduces air resistance, allowing them to conserve their energy
   (b) They make a beautiful pattern and thus look attractive
   (c) This pattern keeps the predators away from the group
   (d) They remain in contact with everyone throughout their long journey

3. Arrange the following animals in the two groups, A–Shy animals and B–Friendly animals;

> Dog, Cow, Squirrel, Deer, Bear, Monkey, Hen, Dolphin

	A	B
(a)	Hen, dolphin, squirrel, deer	Bear, monkey, dog, cow
(b)	Dog, cow, hen, dolphin	Bear, squirrel, dog, cow
(c)	Bear, monkey, dog, cow	Hen, dolphin, squirrel, deer
(d)	Squirrel, deer, bear, monkey	Dog, cow, hen, dolphin

4. Choose the incorrect statement.
   (a) Bears have long hair on skin to keep them warm
   (b) Bears have white skin colour to reflect all the heat
   (c) Bears have a thick layer of fat to protect from cold
   (d) Polar bears have very good sense of smell

5. Given below is the table containing the characteristics of various animals. Choose the animals for which the correct characteristics are mentioned.

Animal	Hair on body	Scales/ feathers	External ears	Internal ears
Fish	Yes	Scales	Yes	Yes
Tiger	Yes	None	Yes	Yes
Sparrow	Yes	Feathers	No	Yes
Snake	Yes	Scales	Yes	Yes

Choose the correct option.
(a) Tiger and sparrow   (b) Tiger and snake
(c) Dolphin and snake   (d) Dolphin and sparrow

Direction (Q. Nos. 6-8) *Read the carefully following passage and answer the questions that follow:*

'Many birds have give and take relationship with some animals. We can see birds sitting on the back of a cow or buffalo and even on back or giraffe and oxen'.

6. Birds riding on cows/buffaloes are called .... and those riding on giraffe/oxen are called as ....
(a) Cattle egrets, giraffe egrets
(b) Ox peckers, cattle egrets
(c) Cattle egrets, ox peckers
(d) Cow peckers, ox peckers

7. What advantage do these birds get from such a relationship?
(a) They get a free ride on their back
(b) They eat insects which lie on skin of these animals
(c) They take rest on their back
(d) They love to be with these animals

8. Match the following animals with their hearing parts.

A. Elephant   (i) Small holes
B. *Hippopotamus* (ii) Big ears
C. Birds   (iii) No ears
D. Snakes   (iv) Small ears

Codes

	A	B	C	D
(a)	(iv)	(i)	(ii)	(iii)
(b)	(iii)	(iv)	(i)	(ii)
(c)	(ii)	(iv)	(i)	(iii)
(d)	(i)	(ii)	(iii)	(iv)

9. Which of the following animals do not have hair on their skin?

> Fish, Cow, Goat, Snake, Tiger

(a) Fish and snake   (b) Tiger and cow
(c) Fish and tiger   (d) Tiger and snake

10. Satya studied about structure of egg in the class. Then, he draw the diagram, but forgot to label it. Help him label it.

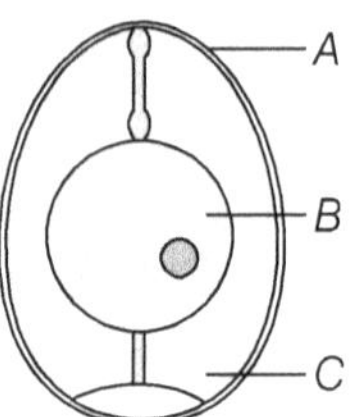

Choose the correct option.

	A	B	C
(a)	Egg membrane	Yolk	Albumin
(b)	Egg shell	Yolk	Albumin
(c)	Egg wall	Albumin	Yolk
(d)	Egg shell	Albumin	Yolk

11. Arrange the following steps of egg hatching in correct sequence.

I. Parent bird sits on the egg to keep it warm.
II. Chick breaks the shell and comes out when grown.
III. Parent bird lays eggs.
IV. Embryo develops into chick.

Codes

(a)	IV	I	II	III
(b)	III	IV	I	II
(c)	III	I	IV	II
(d)	I	II	III	IV

12. What is the difference between a frog's egg and bird's egg?
(a) Frog's egg is bigger than a bird's egg
(b) Frog's egg has a sticky covering for protection, whereas bird's egg has a protective hard shell
(c) Frog's egg is brown in colour, whereas bird's egg is white in colour
(d) All of the above

Direction (Q. Nos. 13-14) *Study the given chart and answer the questions based on it.*

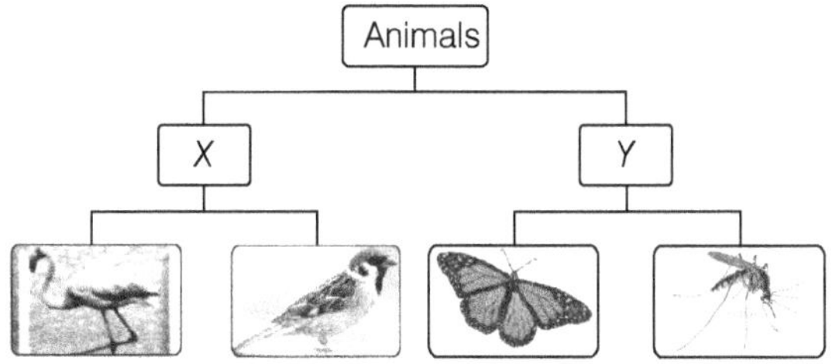

13. What is the similarity between group *X* and group *Y* ?

(a) Both are mammals
(b) Both live in same habitat
(c) Both have same eating habits
(d) Both have wings and can fly

14. What is the difference between group *X* and group *Y* ?

(a) Group *X* lay eggs, group *Y* give birth to young ones
(b) Group *X* has 3 stage life cycle, group *Y* has 4 stage life cycle
(c) Group *X* is big in size, group *Y* is smaller
(d) Group *X* give birth to young ones, group *Y* lay eggs

15. Difference between tadpole and a frog are

(a) tadpole has gills to breathe, frog has lungs
(b) tadpole can live only in water, frog can live both on land and in water
(c) tadpole has a tail, frog has no tail
(d) All of the above

16. Which of the following animals do not take care of their eggs to provide warmth?

Lizard, Sparrow, Hen, Turtle, Snake, Duck

Choose the correct option.

(a) Lizard, turtle, snake
(b) Snake, hen, duck
(c) Lizard, sparrow, duck
(d) Turtle, snake, sparrow

17. Match the following columns.

	Column I		Column II
A.	Reproduction	(i)	Repeated shedding of skin to become an adult
B.	Hatching	(ii)	Process to produce one's own kind
C.	Moulting	(iii)	Breaking of egg shell by chick to come out

Codes

	A	B	C
(a)	(ii)	(iii)	(i)
(b)	(iii)	(ii)	(i)
(c)	(ii)	(iii)	(i)
(d)	(i)	(ii)	(iii)

18. Read the following statements and choose the correct option/s.

Statement A Butterflies do not care for their young ones.

Statement B Their eggs have gelatinous covering and no hard shell.

Statement C Butterflies have a four stage life cycle.

(a) Statement A is incorrect, Statement B and C are correct
(b) Statement B is incorrect, Statement A and C are correct
(c) Statement C is incorrect, Statement A and B are correct
(d) All statements are correct

19. Match the following organisms with their young ones.

A. Cockroach   (i) Tadpole
B. Butterfly   (ii) Chick
C. Frog   (iii) Nymph
D. Bird   (iv) Cocoon

Codes

	A	B	C	D
(a)	(iv)	(i)	(ii)	(iii)
(b)	(iii)	(iv)	(i)	(ii)
(c)	(ii)	(iv)	(i)	(iii)
(d)	(i)	(ii)	(iii)	(iv)

20. A camel lives in the desert, a hot and dry place that gets very little rainfall. Which of the following is not their adaptation to survive in such conditions?

(a) They can store food in form of fat in its hump and stores water in its stomach
(b) They have thick lips so it can eat prickly desert plants without feeling pain
(c) They have black skin colour, so that it absorbs more sun's heat to keep the body warm
(d) They have long eyelashes and extra transparent eyelid to get rid of sand of the desert

21. Which of the following characteristic does not help birds in flying?
    (a) They have hollow bones which makes their body lighter
    (b) They have wings and feathers
    (c) They have streamlined body
    (d) They have beak but not teeth

22. All mammals give birth to young ones except *Platypus* which lay eggs. Then, due to which of the following characteristic, they justify to be a mammal?
    (a) Have lungs to breathe
    (b) Have hairs all over their body
    (c) Have gills to breathe
    (d) Have scales on their body

23. Match the following organisms as per their eating habits.

    A. Dog   (i) Carnivore
    B. Leech   (ii) Herbivore
    C. Elephant   (iii) Omnivore
    D. Lion   (iv) Parasite

    Codes

	A	B	C	D
(a)	(iv)	(i)	(ii)	(iii)
(b)	(iii)	(iv)	(ii)	(i)
(c)	(ii)	(iv)	(i)	(iii)
(d)	(i)	(ii)	(iii)	(iv)

24. Consider the following statements as true or false and choose the correct option.
    I. Camouflage and mimicry are the adaptation of animals to protect themselves from predators.
    II. Tortoise store poisonous substances to protect them.
    III. Monarch butterfly has a hard shell that protects its soft parts.
    IV. Animals like elephant, whale, shark are quite big to have no natural enemies.

    Codes

	I	II	III	IV
(a)	True	True	False	False
(b)	False	False	True	True
(c)	True	False	True	False
(d)	True	False	False	True

25. The diagram below depicts life cycle of a butterfly. Identify different stages of its life correctly and choose the correct option.

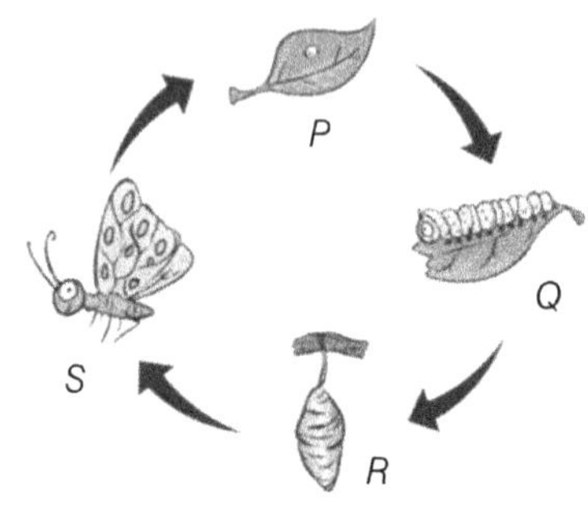

    Codes

	P	Q	R	S
(a)	Egg	Larva	Pupa	Adult
(b)	Adult	Egg	Larva	Pupa
(c)	Pupa	Adult	Egg	Larva
(d)	Larva	Pupa	Adult	Egg

26. In the particular part(s) of the year, many animals move from one place to another for different reasons. Why do you think these animals especially birds, migrate?
    (a) Looking for food
    (b) Escaping the extreme seasonal temperatures
    (c) Moving to breeding grounds to lay eggs
    (d) All of the above

27. Arrange these different stages of life cycle of frog in correct sequence.

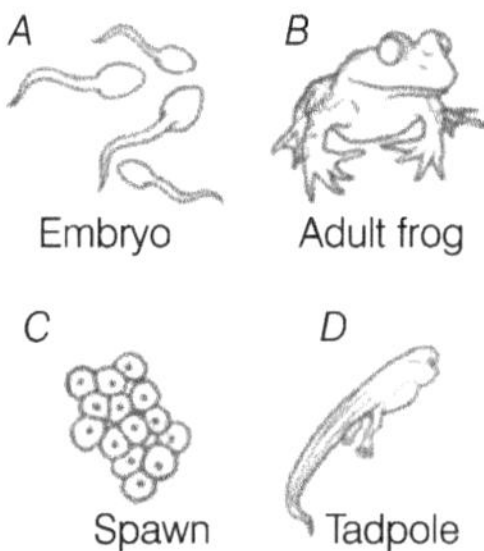

    Choose the correct option.
    (a) $A \to B \to C \to D$
    (b) $D \to C \to B \to A$
    (c) $C \to A \to D \to B$
    (d) $A \to D \to B \to C$

Science Olympiad Class IV

28. Solve the following crossword using hints given below:

Down

1. Group of owls is called as ....
   (a) parliament
   (b) cormorants
   (c) ptarmigans
   (d) convocation

2. .... makes the longest migration.
   (a) Black eagle
   (b) Arctic tern
   (c) Humpy whale
   (d) Jungle myna

Across

3. It is the long mouth part of butterfly to suck nectar from flowers.
   (a) Spiracles
   (b) Wing veins
   (c) Proboscis
   (d) Hibroscis

4. .... is the ability of living things to adjust or adapt to their surroundings.
   (a) Adaptation
   (b) Scratching
   (c) Alteration
   (d) Camouflage

5. .... are friendly sea creatures.
   (a) Blow fish
   (b) Arapaina
   (c) Albacore
   (d) Dolphins

6. Tadpole of frog eat tiny plants called .... in their surroundings.
   (a) algae
   (b) shrub
   (c) herbs
   (d) grass

29. A bird which makes its nest by sowing two leaves together

   (a) Talous
   (b) Weaver bird
   (c) Tailor bird
   (d) Parrot

30. A bird which comes to India to bread in winter
   (a) Pigeon
   (b) Atlantic duck
   (c) Australian hen
   (d) Siberian crane

Plants

1. Choose the incorrect statement.
   (a) Life is possible even without plants on Earth
   (b) Plants make their own food
   (c) There will be no food on Earth without green plants
   (d) Plants are primary source of food for all organisms

2. In what way does the food prepared by plant is used?
   (a) Some food is used by plants to grow
   (b) Some food is used by plants to repair damaged parts
   (c) Extra food is stored as starch and eaten by animals and humans
   (d) All of the above

Direction (Q. Nos. 3-5) *Given are the various steps (jumbled up), taken to carry out test for the presence of starch in a leaf.*

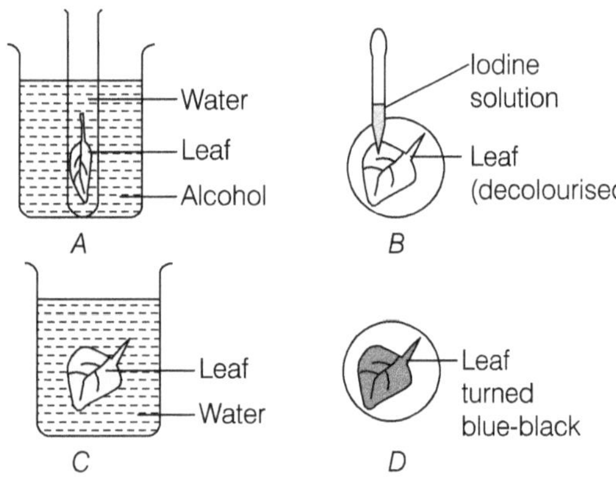

3. Arrange given steps in correct sequence.
   (a) C, A, B, D
   (b) A, B, C, D
   (c) D, C, B, A
   (d) B, A, D, C

4. Why do we need double boiler to heat leaf in alcohol and why can't we heat alcohol directly over flame?
   (a) Reaction is so quick that we cannot judge the timing
   (b) Alcohol could catch fire, as it is inflammable
   (c) To avoid shrinkage of leaves
   (d) To keep the green colour of the leaf intact

5. What is the role of alcohol in this experiment?
   (a) To remove chlorophyll from leaf, i.e. bleaching
   (b) To soften the leaf
   (c) To kill the living cells of leaf
   (d) To burn the leaf

6. Why does leaf turns blue-black on addition of iodine solution?
   (a) Iodine burns the leaf
   (b) Due to the presence of protein, iodine turns leaf to blue-black
   (c) Iodine turns starch blue-black, so it confirms the presence of starch
   (d) To show the absence of starch in the leaf

7. While testing that sunlight is essential for photosynthesis, why is it required to keep the plant in dark place for a day?

    (a) So that leaves will not be able to make food during this time due to the absence of sunlight and will utilise all their stored food

    (b) So that leaves have rest of one day from the number of activities they perform whole day for the plant

    (c) So that leaves lose their colour and become colourless

    (d) All of the above

8. Surya covered one leaf of a plant by black paper for 3-4 days. After that he tested the leaf and other leaves for the presence of starch in them. The leaf covered with black paper does not turn blue-black on addition of iodine solution whereas, all other leaves turned blue-black. Why?

    (a) Black paper absorbed all the starch of that leaf

    (b) Black paper absorbed chlorophyll from leaf so it couldn't perform photosynthesis

    (c) Black paper doesn't allow sunlight to reach leaf so it couldn't perform photosynthesis

    (d) Starch evaporated from that leaf

9. These structures are present on the surface of leaves of plants. From them, plants exchange gases and get rid of excess water. What are these structures called as?

    (a) Stomata

    (b) Veins

    (c) Buds

    (d) All of the above

Direction (Q. Nos. 10-11) *Read the following statements carefully and answer the questions that follow:*

Statement A Chlorophyll is present in leaves and is necessary for photosynthesis.

Statement B *Cactus* does not have leaves.

Statement C Few crotons are red in colour.

10. How does *Cactus* get its food?

    (a) It depends on other plants for food

    (b) It is an insectivorous plant

    (c) Its stem is green and waxy and prepares food for the plant

    (d) It does not need food, as it can survive on atmospheric gases

11. Red colour of crotons does not mean that they do not perform photosynthesis. How?

    (a) Croton plants are green, but do not contain chlorophyll

    (b) Croton plants are special plants whose red pigment participate in photosynthesis

    (c) Croton plants have chlorophyll, but its hidden by dark red colour

    (d) Croton plants can change their colour to green during some part of the day to do photosynthesis

Direction (Q. Nos. 12-13) *The diagram given below shows the classification of plants. Study the diagram carefully and answer the questions that follow:*

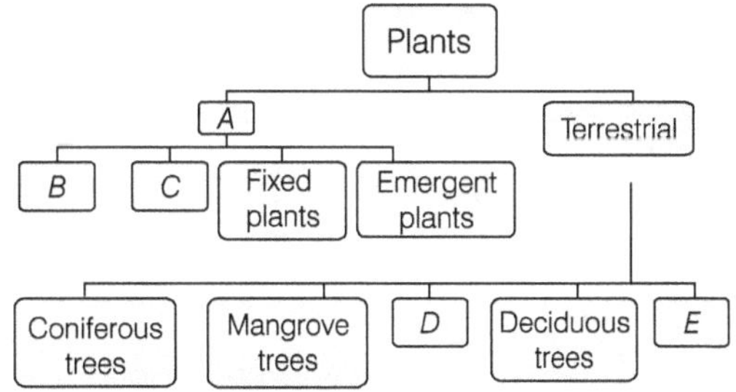

12. What would come in *A*?

    (a) Aquatic plants   (b) Aerial plants

    (c) Desert plants   (d) None of these

13. What will come in *B, C, D* and *E*?

	B	C	D	E
(a)	Free-floating	Under water	Desert plants	Evergreen trees
(b)	Ever floating	Under water	Cruciferous trees	Evergreen trees
(c)	Non-emergent	Free-floating	Deciferous trees	Seasonal trees
(d)	Over water	Under water	Ever seasonal trees	Seasonal trees

14. Why there are no plants beyond 20 m depth under water?

    (a) They cannot respire in such great depth

    (b) Plants need sunlight to prepare food and moreover sunlight can only reach up to depth of 20 m

    (c) No man can go to such depth again and again to sow seeds of different plants

    (d) All of the above

15. How are roots of carrot useful to the plant?

    I. It gives the plant its colour.

    II. Absorbs water and minerals from soil.

    III. Transports water and minerals to all parts of the plant.

    IV. They store food for the plant.

Choose the correct option.

(a) I and II   (b) II and IV
(c) I, II and III   (d) II and III

16. Hollow leaves of this plant are filled with nectar. When insects come to drink this nectar, lid closes and they are eaten by the plant. This plant is

(a) lotus
(b) pitcher plant
(c) venus fly trap
(d) water hyacinth

17. Match the type of terrestrial plants with their specific features.

A.	Coniferous trees	(i)	Remain evergreen
B.	Mangrove trees	(ii)	Have cones instead of flowers
C.	Evergreen trees	(iii)	Shed their leaves in winter
D.	Deciduous trees	(iv)	Have breathing roots

Codes

	A	B	C	D
(a)	(ii)	(iv)	(i)	(iii)
(b)	(i)	(ii)	(iii)	(iv)
(c)	(iv)	(iii)	(ii)	(i)
(d)	(iii)	(ii)	(iv)	(i)

18. 'A plant can be divided into two parts. The part of the plant which grows above the soil, is known as shoot system. The part which grows below the soil is known as root system'.

Which parts form root system and shoot system of the plant?

	Root system	Shoot system
(a)	Root	Leaves, flowers and stem
(b)	Flowers	Roots, leaves and stem
(c)	Leaves	Flowers, roots and stem
(d)	Stem	Roots, flowers and leaves

19. Carrot, radish, turnip and beat root are special type of roots and have been given a unique name due to the role they play. What role do they play and what are they known as?

(a) They go deep into the soil to get water and are known as desert plants
(b) They store food for the plant and are known as storage roots
(c) They are coloured and impart colour to the plant, therefore known as colour roots
(d) They are green in colour and prepare food for the plant and are known as kitchen roots

20. Rahul visited a forest and there he saw a tree with root-like structure growing down from its branches. He got confused and asked his teacher about the tree. His teacher gave him a satisfactory reply, which you have to choose from the following options.

(a) They are storage roots which store food for the plant
(b) They are ropes, hanging down from trees to play by making swings
(c) These trees have inverted structures, roots above, whereas fruits and flowers inside the soil
(d) They have roots which grow downwards from branches to the soil and are known as aerial roots

21. Which of the following is not an adaptive feature of desert plant to survive?

(a) Leaves are reduced to spines to prevent loss of water
(b) Long roots are present, which go deeper in the soil in search of water
(c) They are colourless plants and do not do photosynthesis, thus saving water
(d) None of the above

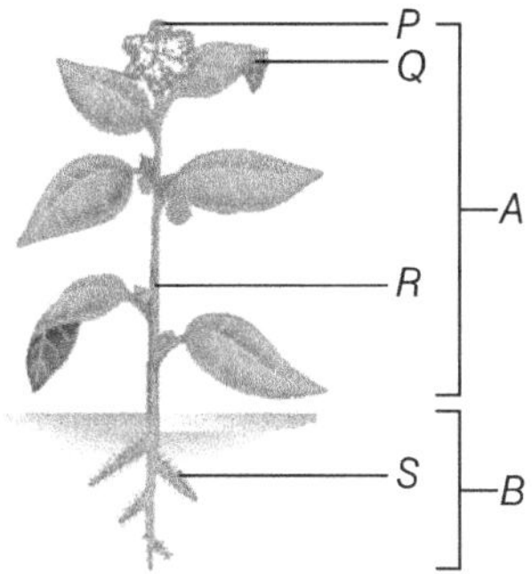

22. What is *A* and *B*?
- (a) *A*—Root system;   *B*—Shoot system
- (b) *A*—Shoot system;   *B*—Root system
- (c) *A*—Upper parts;   *B*—Lower parts
- (d) *A*—Stem system;   *B*—Water system

23. What are the labels *P*, *Q*, *R* and *S*?

	P	Q	R	S
(a)	Flower	Roots	Leaves	Stem
(b)	Leaves	Flower	Roots	Stem
(c)	Roots	Leaves	Flower	Stem
(d)	Flower	Leaves	Stem	Roots

24. Roots of a plant grow deep inside the soil. They hold the plant firmly to the soil. They can be of two types. Identify them in the diagram given below:

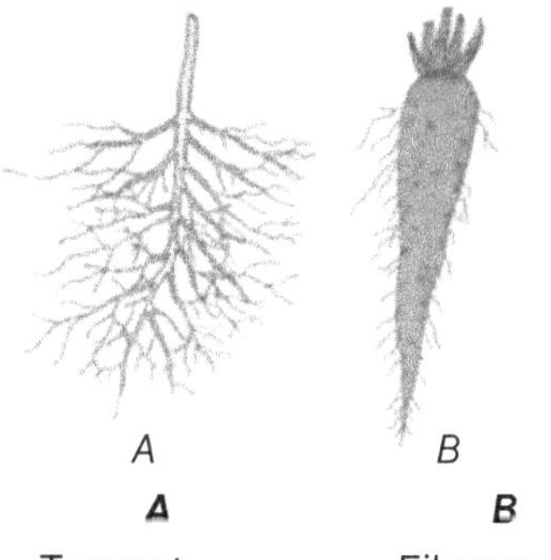

(a)	Tap root	Fibrous root
(b)	Fibrous root	Tap root
(c)	Evergreen roots	Desert roots
(d)	Desert roots	Evergreen roots

Direction (Q. Nos. 25 -26) *Read the following information and picture and answer the questions that follow:*

Plant *A* does not grow on soil and also they do not prepare their own food as they cannot absorb water from soil. They grow on trees as shown in the picture.

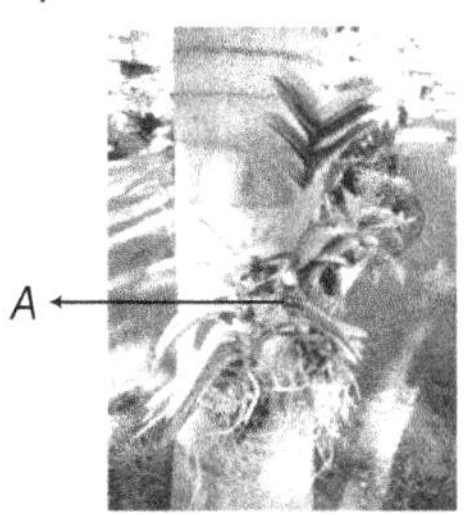

25. How does this plant *A* survive?
- (a) They take food and water from the stem of the tree to grow
- (b) They take food and water from the air by their aerial roots
- (c) Gardener has to artificially supply them with food and water
- (d) All of the above

26. What are such plants known as?
- (a) Insectivorous plants
- (b) Non-green plants
- (c) Dependent plants
- (d) Parasitic plants

Direction (Q. Nos. 27-28) *Answer the questions based on the pictures given below:*

27. What appears first on the plant and develops into second-one?
- (a) Bud appears first and develops into a flower
- (b) Flower appears first and develops into a bud
- (c) Both appears at the same time
- (d) Fruits appear first and develops into bud and flower

28. Label *X* and *Y* part of the flower.
   (a) *X*—Sepal   *Y*—Petal
   (b) *X*—Petal   *Y*—Sepal
   (c) *X*—Leaves   *Y*—Petal
   (d) *X*—Fruits   *Y*—Leaves

29. Complete the following crossword using hints given below:

Across

1. .... plants grow in soil which are poor in minerals and so they eat insects for nutrition.
   (a) Insectivorous   (b) Mediterranean
   (c) Brillantaisia   (d) Cochlospermum

2. .... are the tiny openings in the leaf between cells.
   (a) Air sacs   (b) Bubbles
   (c) Stomata   (d) Pin hole

Down

3. Paper was first made by people of egypt from a grass called ....
   (a) *Sachrus*
   (b) *Angsana*
   (c) *Sandbur*
   (d) *Papyrus*

4. Flowers of a plant contains .... , which honeybees suck.
   (a) nectar   (b) toxins
   (c) liquid   (d) poison

5. .... flower smell like a rotten fish.
   (a) Alang   (b) Orchid
   (c) Corpse   (d) Deodar

6. Farms or place where bees are kept to obtain honey.
   (a) Apiaries   (b) Beeswarm
   (c) Orchards   (d) Beehives

30. Look at this picture and give a word for the process?

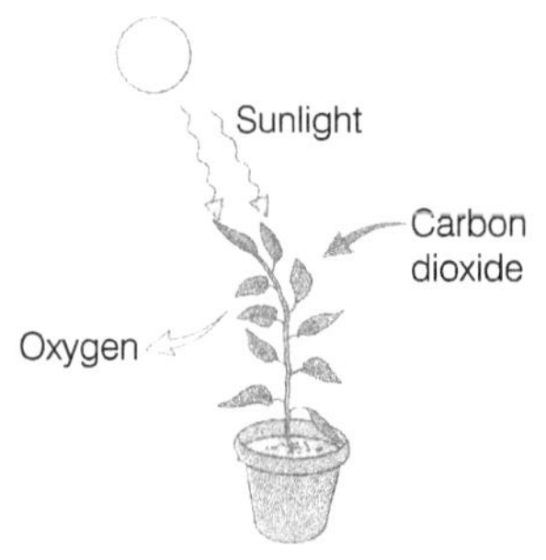

   (a) Venation
   (b) Chlorophyll
   (c) Photosynthesis
   (d) None of the above

Livings, Transportation and Communication

Topic A – Living

1. Which of the following houses shown in figures below is pucca house?

I.  II. 

III. 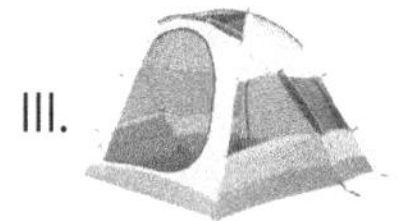 IV. 

Codes
(a) Only II
(b) II and III
(c) Only I
(d) I and IV

2. Choose the incorrect statement in context with shelter and habitat.
(a) People make their houses as per the climate of a particular area
(b) People living in snow covered regions prefer to live in igloos
(c) People living in earthquake prone areas prefer to live in tents
(d) All of the above

3. While watching an episode on Antarctica on discovery channel, Daniel was amazed to see the white houses of that area. What type of houses would they be?
(a) Stilt house
(b) Pucca house
(c) Igloo
(d) Hut

4. Figure shown below depicts a house whose parts are marked with A, B, C and D.

Which of the following option correctly label the parts?

	A	B	C	D
(a)	Window	Ceiling	Door	Wall
(b)	Ceiling	Window	Wall	Door
(c)	Wall	Door	Ceiling	Window
(d)	Wall	Door	Window	Ceiling

5. Match the given matrix in context with the type of rooms given in figures below:

A.    (i)   Drawing room

B.    (ii)   Bathroom

C.    (iii)   Kitchen

D.    (iv)   Bedroom

E.    (v)   Dining room

Codes

	A	B	C	D	E
(a)	(iv)	(iii)	(v)	(i)	(ii)
(b)	(i)	(ii)	(iii)	(iv)	(v)
(c)	(v)	(iv)	(iii)	(ii)	(i)
(d)	(iii)	(iv)	(ii)	(v)	(i)

6. Consider the following statements and state true (T)/false (F) using options given below:

   I. An igloo can be found in snow covered areas only.

   II. Stilt houses are made of snow.

   III. House boats are used by tourists during vacations.

   IV. Tents and stilt houses are permanent houses.

   V. Houses with sloped roof are found in places having heavy rainfall.

Codes

	I	II	III	IV	V
(a)	F	T	F	T	F
(b)	T	F	T	F	T
(c)	F	F	F	T	T
(d)	T	T	F	F	F

7. Complete the passage using suitable words given in options below:

People prefer to live in ......*A*...... . Just like us, animals and ......*B*...... also have their ......*C*...... . A habitat is a special ......*D*...... where a plant or animal ......*E*...... .

Codes

	A	B	C	D	E
(a)	plants	habitats	societies	lives	place
(b)	societies	plants	habitats	place	lives
(c)	habitats	place	societies	plants	lives
(d)	houses	societies	plants	lives	place

Direction (Q. Nos. 8-9) *Read the following information carefully and answer the questions that follow:*

Any place which is being used by a living being for its accommodation is a house. Houses today are made up of strong and durable materials like bricks and cement. These materials last for a long time and require less repairs. Walls are usually plastered with cement. Materials like glass and plywood are used for doors and windows.

8. Which of the following is not a material used to make a house?

  (a) Cement   (b) Glass

  (c) Wood   (d) Cloth

9. What could be the most appropriate reason for houses being made of strong and durable materials?

  (a) To make them look beautiful

  (b) To increase the cost of maintenance

  (c) To decrease the cost of maintenance

  (d) The materials are cheaply available

10. Metro trains running across major cities is which mode of transport?

(a) Roadways   (b) Railways

(c) Trainways   (d) Land transport

11. The roads which are constructed to join major cities of a country are known as

(a) Grand trunk road   (b) National highway

(c) Both (a) and (b)   (d) Either (a) or (b)

12. Choose the incorrect statement in context with transportation.

  I. Animals like camel and bullock are means of road transport.

  II. Railways consume less time as compared to roadways and airways.

  III. Ships can be used to cross a sea or river.

Choose the correct option.

(a) Only III   (b) Only I

(c) Only II   (d) All of these

13. Match the given matrix in context with the type of transport.

A. Airways   (i)

Autorickshaw

B. Railways   (ii)

Ship

C. Waterways   (iii)

Helicopter

D. Roadways   (iv)

Metro train

Codes

	A	B	C	D
(a)	(i)	(ii)	(iii)	(iv)
(b)	(iii)	(iv)	(ii)	(i)
(c)	(iv)	(iii)	(i)	(ii)
(d)	(ii)	(i)	(iv)	(iii)

14. Consider the following statements and state true (T)/false (F) by choosing the options given below:

  I. Highways are the ways which are used to travel by trains.

  II. Waterways are the cheapest mode of transport.

  III. Trains run on specially made tracks laid down along fields.

  IV. Now-a-days bullock carts are run using CNG.

  V. Roadways and railways are land transports.

Codes

	I	II	III	IV	V
(a)	F	T	T	F	T
(b)	T	F	F	T	F
(c)	F	F	F	T	T
(d)	T	T	T	F	F

15. Complete the passage using suitable words given in the options below:

......A...... are one of the oldest type of ......B...... . People use to travel through rivers and seas to ......C...... their goods in other parts of the world. In many parts of the country, animals like ......D...... , elephant and camel are also being used as a ......E...... of transportation.

Codes

	A	B	C	D	E
(a)	Aero-plane	transpor-tation	market	bullock	means
(b)	Camel	commu-nication	trade	elephant	means
(c)	Bullock	shelter	market	camel	way
(d)	Boats	transport	trade	bullock	means

16. It is a two wheeled carriage, which is drawn by a single horse.

(a) Bullock cart

(b) Buggy

(c) Tonga

(d) None of the above

17. Match the following columns.

	Column I		Column II
A.	Camel carts	(i)	Mountain
B.	Bullock carts	(ii)	Battle field
C.	Yaks and ponies	(iii)	Desert
D.	Elephants	(iv)	Town market

Codes

	A	B	C	D
(a)	(i)	(iv)	(iii)	(ii)
(b)	(iii)	(iv)	(i)	(ii)
(c)	(i)	(ii)	(iv)	(iii)
(d)	(iii)	(ii)	(i)	(iv)

Topic C – Communication

18. Which of the following figures shown below is not a means of communication?

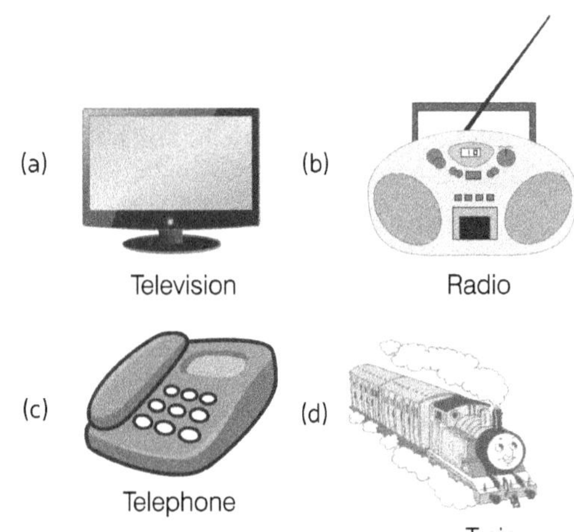

19. Which one of them shown in figures below represents a source of mass communication?

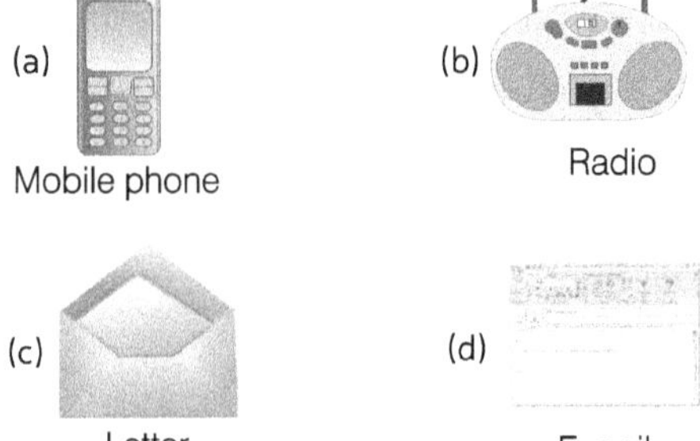

20. In order to convey a message through all over a city, Shikha wants to use print media. Which of the following can she consider?

I. Television
II. Newspaper
III. Radio
IV. Magazines
V. Internet

Choose the correct option.

(a) I, II and III   (b) III, IV and V
(c) II and IV   (d) II, IV and V

21. Which of the following is the most appropriate way to send an urgent message?
(a) Money order
(b) Speed post
(c) Postcard
(d) Parcel

22. Faiz wants to send his vacation pics to his friend who lives in other state. Which of the following would be the fastest and cheapest mode of communication for him?
(a) Courier   (b) Speed post
(c) E-mail   (d) FAX

23. Match the given matrix as per the correct abbreviations given in columns below:

	Column I		Column II
A.	E-mail	(i)	Facsimile Automated Xerox
B.	FAX	(ii)	Around Indian Radio
C.	www	(iii)	All India Radio
D.	AIR	(iv)	Electrical Mail
		(v)	Fast Automatic Xerox
		(vi)	Electronic Mail
		(vii)	World Web Wide
		(viii)	World Wide Web

Codes

	A	B	C	D
(a)	(vi)	(v)	(viii)	(ii)
(b)	(iv)	(v)	(vii)	(ii)
(c)	(iv)	(i)	(vii)	(iii)
(d)	(vi)	(i)	(viii)	(iii)

24. Complete the passage using suitable words given in the option below:

......*A*...... communication plays a crucial role in creating ......*B*...... among the people. It can deliver a ......*C*...... to a mass at a time. ......*D*...... and ......*E*...... are some examples of mass communication.

Codes

	A	B	C	D	E
(a)	Wide	mass	news	book	communication
(b)	Magazine	newspaper	book	newspaper	news
(c)	TV	message	awareness	television	magazine
(d)	Mass	awareness	message	newspapers	television

25. State true (T) or false (F) using the options given below:

I. If a person needs to make a call to another person living in other city, then the call is ISD.

II. ISD calls are made between two countries.

III. STD stands for Subscriber Trunk Dialing.

IV. STD calls are made between two countries.

V. Telegram is the fastest means of communication.

Codes

	I	II	III	IV	V
(a)	T	F	F	T	T
(b)	F	T	T	F	F
(c)	T	T	F	F	T
(d)	F	T	F	F	T

Direction (Q. Nos. 26-27) *Read the following information carefully and answer the questions that follow:*

Communication refers to transmission of ideas from one person to another. Communication can be personal as well as mass communication. Personal communication includes telephone, telegram, e-mail, etc. Mass communication includes newspapers, radio, television, etc.

26. What do you understand by communication?
(a) Transferring money from one person to another
(b) Transferring data from one person to another
(c) Transferring views from one person to another
(d) All of the above

27. Which of the following options does not depict the type of communication matched correctly?
(a) Telephone– Personal communication
(b) Newspaper– Mass communication
(c) E-mail– Mass communication
(d) Television– Mass communication

28. Name the mode of communication which is used by government to create awareness?
(a) FAX　　(b) Telegram　(c) Radio　　(d) E-mail

29. In ancient times, people used .... for transport.
(a) wheel　　(b) carts　　(c) animals　(d) birds

30. We share our homes with some unwanted visitors. They are called as ....
(a) birds　　(b) animals　(c) pests　　(d) snacks

Our Body

1. Normal human heart beats at a regular rate which determines healthy working of the heart. What is that?
   (a) 72 times in a min
   (b) 120 times in a min
   (c) 50 times in a min
   (d) 90 times in a min

2. Food pipe and wind pipe lies parallel. Then also when we eat food, it does not enters into the wind pipe. Which structure prevents entry of food into wind pipe?
   (a) Epiglottis
   (b) Trachea
   (c) Oesophagus
   (d) Larynx

3. 'Blood flows through blood vessels'. What is the function of blood vessels?
   (a) They carry blood from heart to body parts
   (b) They carry blood from body parts to heart
   (c) Both (a) and (b)
   (d) None of the above

4. Rib cage protects sensitive organs like heart and lungs for external injury. How many pairs of ribs are there in this protective structure?
   (a) 12
   (b) 10
   (c) 15
   (d) 8

5. Identify following organs of our body and match with appropriate option.

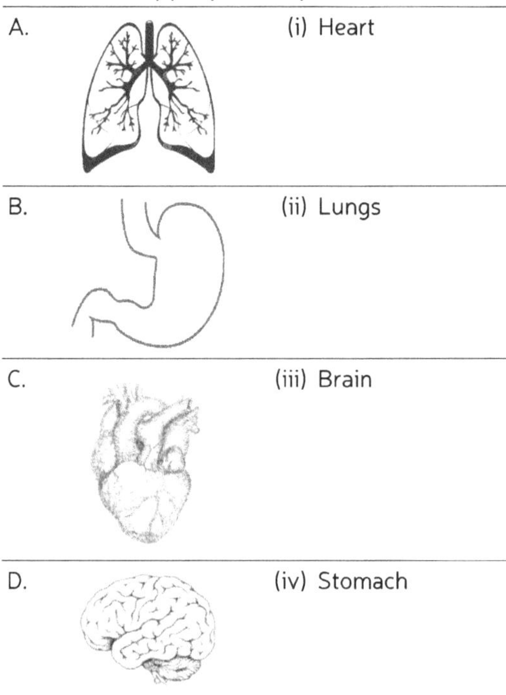

Codes

	A	B	C	D
(a)	(i)	(iii)	(ii)	(iv)
(b)	(iv)	(iii)	(ii)	(i)
(c)	(ii)	(iv)	(i)	(iii)
(d)	(iv)	(ii)	(iii)	(i)

6. Read the following statement and choose the correct option.

   I. Heart beats only sometimes in our life.

   II. We get energy from the food.

   III. Blood carries hydrogen from heart to all body parts.

   IV. Digestion is the process with which we throw our body wastes out.

Codes

	I	II	III	IV
(a)	T	T	F	T
(b)	T	T	F	F
(c)	F	T	F	F
(d)	T	F	T	T

7. Air which we inhale through our nose also has many dust particles along with oxygen. Entering of these dust particles may cause blockage of respiration system. What prevents dust particles getting into the respiratory tract?

(a) Epiglottis
(b) Wind pipe
(c) Small hairs in the nose
(d) Lungs

8. Which of the following depicts correct movement of air through respiratory system?

(a) Lungs → Nose → Pharynx
(b) Nose → Lungs → Pharynx
(c) Nose → Pharynx → Lungs
(d) Pharynx → Nose → Lungs

9. Brain is the control centre of activities that take place in our body. Which of the following activities are controlled by brain?

(a) Walking   (b) Talking
(c) Swallowing   (d) All of these

10. Match the following columns.

A.	Digestion	(i)	Removal of waste from the body.
B.	Excretion	(ii)	Flow of blood to different body parts and heart.
C.	Respiration	(iii)	Process of getting nutrients and energy from the food.
D.	Circulation	(iv)	Taking in oxygen and giving out carbon dioxide.

Codes

	A	B	C	D		A	B	C	D
(a)	(i)	(iii)	(ii)	(iv)	(b)	(iv)	(iii)	(ii)	(i)
(c)	(iii)	(i)	(iv)	(ii)	(d)	(iv)	(ii)	(iii)	(i)

11. 'Digestive system is made up of so many organs which work together to digest food'. In which part of digestive tract, no digestion occurs?

(a) Large intestine   (b) Small intestine
(c) Stomach   (d) Mouth

Direction (Q. Nos. 12-15) *Study the given diagram carefully and answer the following questions.*

12. Complete the given excretory system by filling up *P, Q, R* and *S*.

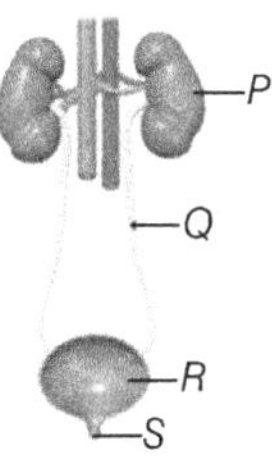

Codes

	P	Q	R	S
(a)	Kidneys	Ureters	Urinary bladder	Urethra
(b)	Urethra	Ureters	Urinary bladder	Kidneys
(c)	Ureters	Urethra	Kidneys	Urinary bladder
(d)	Urethra	Urinary bladder	Ureters	Kidneys

13. Which part of excretory system filters our blood?

(a) *P*   (b) *Q*
(c) *R*   (d) *S*

14. What is the exact location of kidneys?

(a) Below the rib cage   (b) Near heart
(c) Above rib cage   (d) Behind stomach

15. Which of the following are present in pair?

(a) Kidney and ureters
(b) Kidney and urethra
(c) Urethra and urine bladder
(d) Kidney and urine bladder

16. We breathe in oxygen for air and breathe out carbon dioxide. Where does this carbon dioxide come from?
(a) From the blood
(b) From the bones
(c) From the heart
(d) From the kidneys

17. What is represented by *A*? Name the organ.

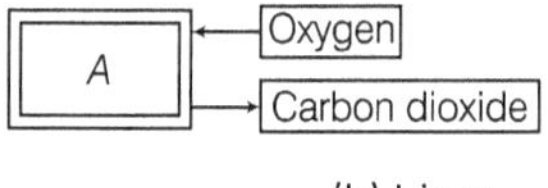

(a) Heart
(b) Liver
(c) Lungs
(d) Brain

18. Match the following columns.

	Column I	Column II
A.	Kidneys	(i) Mosquito biting
B.	Food must be	(ii) Defence system of body
C.	Dengue is caused by	(iii) Clean our blood
D.	Immune system is	(iv) Covered

Codes

	A	B	C	D
(a)	(i)	(iii)	(ii)	(iv)
(b)	(iv)	(iii)	(ii)	(i)
(c)	(iii)	(iv)	(i)	(ii)
(d)	(iv)	(ii)	(iii)	(i)

19. Arrange different steps of excretion in correct order.
I. Urinary bladder temporarily stores urine.
II. Kidneys filter and clear blood from wastes.
III. Water along with waste in form of urine move to ureter.
IV. Urine is passed out of body by urethra.
V. Ureters carry urine from kidneys to urinary bladder.

Codes
(a) II → III → V → I → IV
(b) V → IV → I → III → II
(c) V → IV → III → II → I
(d) IV → III → V → II → I

20. Match the parts of brain with the functions performed by that part.

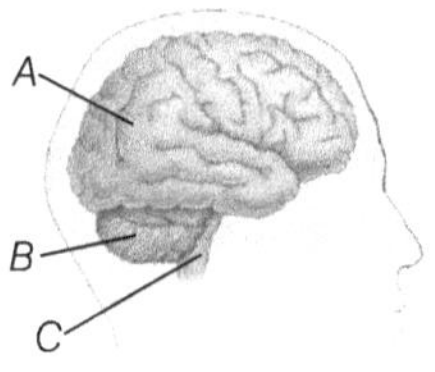

I. It connects brain to spinal cord.
II. It is the centre of intelligence.
III. It controls body movements.

Codes

	A	B	C			A	B	C
(a)	I	II	III		(b)	III	II	I
(c)	II	III	I		(d)	III	I	II

21. Surya learnt respiratory system in school. Next day, when teacher took test, he was able to draw the diagram correctly, but forgot to label certain arts. Help him to complete the diagram.

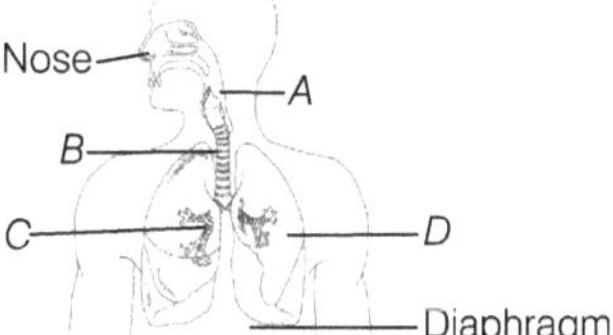

Codes

	A	B	C	D
(a)	Bronchi	Lungs	Pharynx	Trachea
(b)	Trachea	Lungs	Pharynx	Bronchi
(c)	Pharynx	Trachea	Bronchi	Lungs
(d)	Trachea	Pharynx	Lungs	Bronchi

22. Match the following systems of our body with their main body parts and organs.

A.	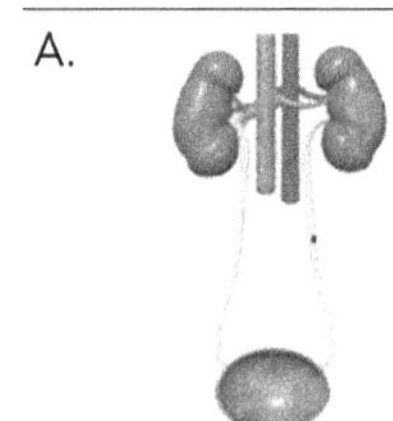	(i) Stomach, liver, pancreas, small intestine and large intestine.

B. 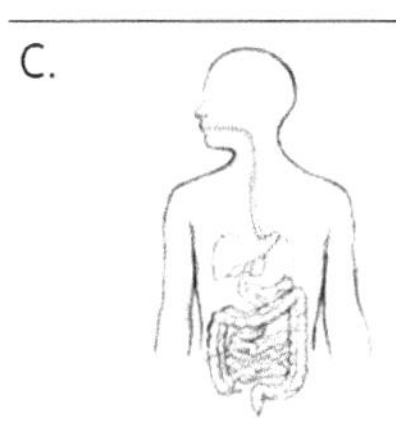   (ii) Pharynx, trachea, lungs and bronchi.

C. 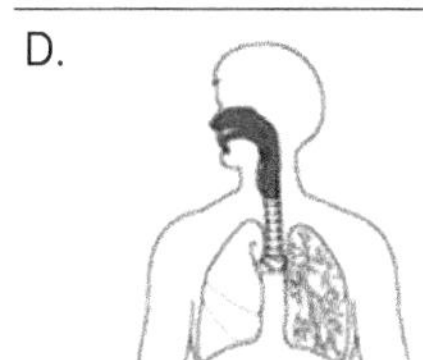   (iii) Kidneys, ureters, urinary bladder and urethra.

D.   (iv) Heart and blood vessels.

Codes

	A	B	C	D		A	B	C	D
(a)	(i)	(iii)	(ii)	(iv)	(b)	(iv)	(iii)	(ii)	(i)
(c)	(iii)	(iv)	(i)	(ii)	(d)	(iv)	(ii)	(iii)	(i)

23. Solve the following crossword using hints given below:

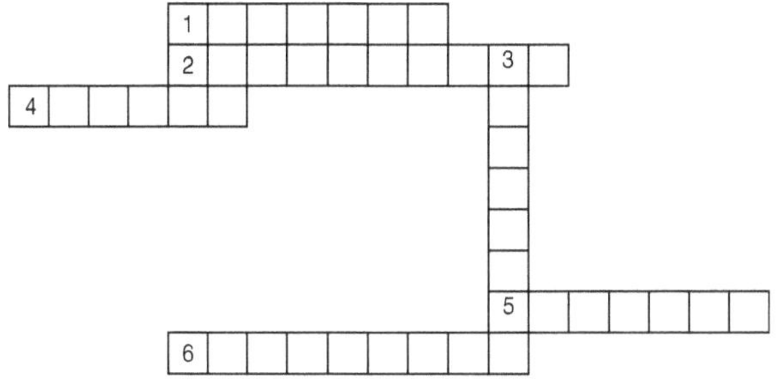

Down

3. In lungs, the .... of gases takes place.
   - (a) transfer
   - (b) exchange
   - (c) shortage
   - (d) eruption

Across

1. .... releases urine outside the body.
   - (a) Urethra
   - (b) Kidneys
   - (c) Ureters
   - (d) Bladder

2. .... of immune system are like weapons of an army.
   - (a) Antibodies
   - (b) Immunisers
   - (c) Agglutinin
   - (d) Lymph nodes

4. .... is responsible for production of sound.
   - (a) Uvular
   - (b) Throat
   - (c) Larynx
   - (d) Palate

5. In stomach, food gets mixed with .... juices that comes from stomach.
   - (a) gastric
   - (b) antigen
   - (c) pylorus
   - (d) vaccine

6. Fingerprints were used as .... in ancient Babylon in second millennium BCE.
   - (a) identity
   - (b) documents
   - (c) character
   - (d) signature

24. Match the activities with the parts of the body these are done with

A.    (i) Feet

B.    (ii) Tongue

C.    (iii) Hands

D.    (iv) Eyes

Codes

	A	B	C	D
(a)	(ii)	(i)	(iii)	(iv)
(b)	(iii)	(ii)	(i)	(iv)
(c)	(iii)	(ii)	(iv)	(i)
(d)	(i)	(ii)	(iii)	(iv)

25. The script which is used by the people who cannot see.

(a) Braille
(b) Sign language
(c) Calipers
(d) None of the above

26. Which among them is not a sense organ?

(a) Legs   (b) Nose
(c) Eyes   (d) Ears

27. How many bones a human body have?

(a) 32   (b) 144
(c) 206   (d) 205

28. What is the main function of tongue?

(a) The tongue helps in digestion
(b) The tongue helps in emulsification
(c) The tongue helps us to speak
(d) None of the above

29. Look at the picture and tell that to which part of the body they used to support?

(a) Legs
(b) Eyes
(c) Hands
(d) Ears

30. Why does callipers used for?

(a) This is a sign language
(b) Children suffering from polio learn to walk with these
(c) This is used for eye disease
(d) This is an ear machine

Food

1. Match the following food grains with the category they belong.

   A. Rice   (i) Pulses
   B. Mustard   (ii) Spices
   C. Cardamom   (iii) Cereals
   D. Black gram   (iv) Oilseed

   Codes

	A	B	C	D
(a)	(i)	(iii)	(ii)	(iv)
(b)	(i)	(ii)	(iii)	(iv)
(c)	(iii)	(iv)	(ii)	(i)
(d)	(iv)	(ii)	(iii)	(i)

2. Arrange the following steps of farming in correct sequence.

   I. Irrigating the crops
   II. Winnowing
   III. Threshing
   IV. Sowing the seeds
   V. Ploughing the field
   VI. Harvesting the crops

   Choose the correct option.
   (a) V → IV → I → VI → III → II
   (b) VI → IV → I → III → II → V
   (c) V → IV → VI → II → I → III
   (d) V → VI → IV → II → I → III

3. Match the following farming processes with their definition.

   A. Harvesting   (i) Removal of husk from grains.
   B. Ploughing   (ii) Separation of grains from plants.
   C. Threshing   (iii) Turning up of soil before sowing seeds.
   D. Winnowing   (iv) Cutting and collection of crops.

   Codes

	A	B	C	D		A	B	C	D
(a)	(ii)	(iii)	(i)	(iv)	(b)	(i)	(ii)	(iii)	(iv)
(c)	(iii)	(iv)	(ii)	(i)	(d)	(iv)	(iii)	(ii)	(i)

4. Complete the process of packing grains.
   Grains are taken from the factory
   ↓

   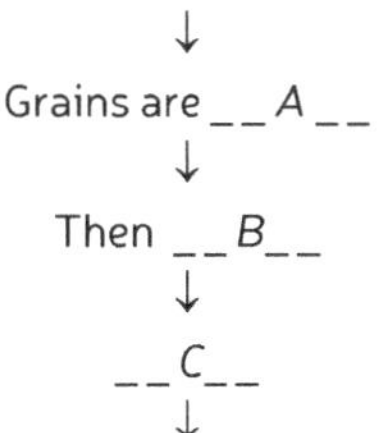

   Grains are _ _ A _ _
   ↓
   Then _ _ B _ _
   ↓
   _ _ C _ _
   ↓

   Sent to wholesale market for sale.

	A	B	C
(a)	Labelled	Cleaned	Packed
(b)	Packed	Cleaned	Labelled
(c)	Cleaned	Packed	Labelled
(d)	Labelled	Packed	Cleaned

5. Arrange the following in correct order. How these people help food grain to reach on doorstep?

I. Truck driver II. Grocer
III. Farmer IV. Worker in mandi

Choose the correct option.

(a) I → II → III → IV
(b) III → I → IV → II
(c) II → IV → I → III
(d) III → II → I → IV

6. Given below is the picture of tongue representing different areas for different tastes. Label them correctly.

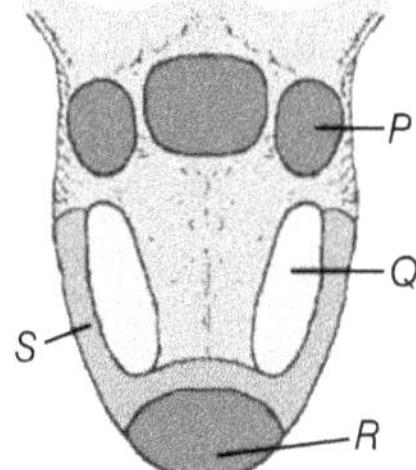

Codes

	P	Q	R	S
(a)	Sweet	Sour	Bitter	Salty
(b)	Sour	Sweet	Salty	Bitter
(c)	Bitter	Sour	Sweet	Salty
(d)	Salty	Bitter	Sour	Sweet

Direction (Q. Nos. 7-8) *Read the following passage and answer the questions that follow:*

'The tongue is an organ that helps us to identify the taste of food we eat. It has tiny bumps on its surface'.

7. What are these tiny bumps on surface of tongue?

(a) Taste corners
(b) Taste points
(c) Taste buds
(d) Taste tips

8. How do tongue senses taste?

(a) Taste buds on tongue have nerves that tell the brain about taste of food
(b) Taste buds on tongue have sensors which can sense taste and tell us
(c) Taste the food and speaks up to tell us what the taste is
(d) None of the above

9. Read the following statements and choose the correct option.

Statement A Tongue helps us to detect the taste of the food.

Statement B Tongue helps us to push chewed food into food pipe.

Statement C Tongue helps us to speak clearly.

(a) Statement A and B are correct; statement C is incorrect
(b) All statements are correct
(c) Statement A and C are correct; statement B is incorrect
(d) Statement B and C are correct; statement A is incorrect

10. Proteins are the ......A...... food, vitamins and minerals are the ......B...... food and fats and carbohydrates are the ......C...... food.

(a) A– Energy giving B– Body building
C– Protective
(b) A– Height providing B– Protective C– Fat giving
(c) A– Body building B– Protective
C– Energy giving
(d) A– Energy building B– Body building
C– Protective

11. Match vitamins with their uses.

A. Vitamin-A (i) Makes teeth and bones strong
B. Vitamin-B (ii) Makes gums strong and heals wounds faster
C. Vitamin-C (iii) Good for muscles and nerves
D. Vitamin-D (iv) Keeps eyes and skin healthy

Codes

	A	B	C	D		A	B	C	D
(a)	(i)	(iii)	(ii)	(iv)	(b)	(iv)	(iii)	(ii)	(i)
(c)	(iii)	(iv)	(ii)	(i)	(d)	(iv)	(ii)	(iii)	(i)

12. Here are few facts about water and its importance in our body. Which one is not correct about water?

(a) About 95% of our body is made up of water
(b) We lose lots of water through urine and sweat
(c) Water helps to maintain our body temperature
(d) We should drink atleast 6-8 glasses of water per day

13. What are protective food?

I. Green leafy vegetables II. Potatoes
III. Milk and milk product IV. Pulses

Direction (Q. Nos. 14-17) *Observe the given diagram carefully and answer the questions based on it.*

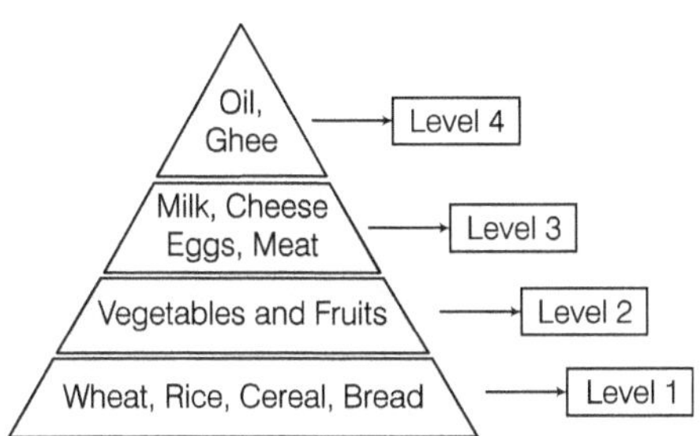

14. The food items in Level 1 are rich in
(a) protein   (b) carbohydrates
(c) fat   (d) vitamins

15. The primary function of level three component is
(a) to give energy
(b) to give warmth to the body
(c) to build and repair parts of the body
(d) to build stronger bones

16. Which of the following table representing different levels and the main constituents in the food items of that level is true?

	Level 1	Level 2	Level 3	Level 4
(a)	Carbo-hydrates	Vitamins and minerals	Proteins	Fats
(b)	Fats	Carbo-hydrates	Proteins	Vitamins and minerals
(c)	Vitamins and minerals	Fats	Carbo-hydrates	Proteins
(d)	Proteins	Vitamins and minerals	Fats	Carbo-hydrates

17. To get quick energy .... foods should be taken more.
(a) Level 1
(b) Level 2
(c) Level 3
(d) Level 4

Direction (Q. No. 18) *Observe the figure of a person given below and answer the questions based on it.*

18. What would you call the condition of this person?
(a) Obesity   (b) Headache
(c) Malaria   (d) Anaemia

19. Look at the picture and tell us why we should not eat food from this stall. Because it contains......

I. Germs   II. Mosquitoes
III. Dust   IV. Flies
Codes
(a) I and II   (b) I, III and IV
(c) Only II   (d) II and III

20. Shobit want to prepare a project on digestive system. He wrote different steps on paper and cut those slips to paste them in scrapbook. But he forgot the correct order. Help him to arrange those steps in correct order.
I. Digested food passes, then wall of small intestine to blood.
II. Food enters stomach where mashed food changes into semi-solid form.
III. Churned food from mouth enters oesophagus.
IV. Liquid food moves to small intestine.
V. Undigested food and water enters large intestine and finally passes out through anus.
VI. Liver, gall bladder and pancreas help small intestine to complete digest of food.

Choose the correct option.

(a) III → II → IV → I → VI → V
(b) I → III → II → V → IV → VI
(c) V → VI → II → IV → III → I
(d) VI → I → III → IV → II → V

21. Help him in completing the labelling of the diagram.

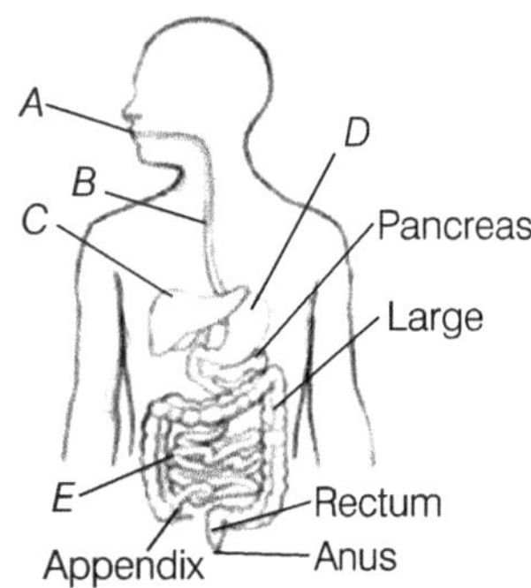

	A	B	C	D	E
(a)	Liver	Stomach	Oeso-phagus	Mouth	Small intestine
(b)	Small intestine	Liver	Mouth	Oeso-phagus	Stomach
(c)	Small intestine	Mouth	Stomach	Liver	Oeso-phagus
(d)	Mouth	Oeso-phagus	Liver	Stomach	Small intestine

22. Also answer this question based on the above diagram. In which part of digestive system undigested food is stored?

(a) Stomach   (b) Large intestine
(c) Anus   (d) Pancreas

23. For proper digestion of food,

  I. we should have food at random hours of time.

  II. we should eat balanced food.

  III. we should eat slowly and chew food well.

  IV. we should not overeat.

Choose the correct option.

	I	II	III	IV		I	II	III	IV
(a)	T	T	T	F	(b)	T	T	F	F
(c)	F	F	T	T	(d)	F	T	T	T

24. How can following food items be preserved?

A. Milk   (i) Dehydration
B. Meat   (ii) Salting
C. Pickles   (iii) Freezing
D. Peas   (iv) Boiling

Codes

	A	B	C	D		A	B	C	D
(a)	(i)	(iii)	(ii)	(iv)	(b)	(ii)	(iii)	(iv)	(i)
(c)	(iii)	(iv)	(ii)	(i)	(d)	(iv)	(iii)	(ii)	(i)

25. Solve the following crossword using hints given below :

Across

1. Tea and coffee are common ……… .
   (a) junk foods   (b) beverages
   (c) voluntary   (d) minerals

2. ……… is the process of breaking down of food into simpler substances so, that it can be used by the body.
   (a) Digestion (b) Ingestion (c) Attrition (d) Blendings

Down

3. The thin layer of food gets deposited on teeth and gradually becomes yellow. This layer is called ……… .
   (a) plaque   (b) badge   (c) grease   (d) trophy

4. Undigested food passes from large intestine into the ……… .
   (a) kidney   (b) nerves   (c) rectum   (d) bowels

5. Langar is served in ………… .
   (a) gurudwara   (b) marriages
   (c) hospitals   (d) birthdays

6. A ……… can have up to 3000 teeth.
   (a) whale   (b) crook   (c) kerry   (d) shark

CHAPTER 7

Our Universe

1. Arrange the objects given below in increasing order of their size.

   I. Star   II. Galaxy

   III. Solar system   IV. Planet

   Choose the correct option.
   - (a) II, III, I, IV
   - (b) III, IV, II, I
   - (c) I, IV, III, II
   - (d) IV, I, III, II

2. Why is it not possible to see Moon and stars during daytime?
   - (a) The Moon and stars hide behind the clouds during daytime
   - (b) The bright sunlight does not allow to see Moon and stars
   - (c) The Moon and stars does not emit light during daytime
   - (d) All of the above

3. I am blue and green. I am small too with life all around. I don't have many Moons but one. Who am I?
   - (a) Mars
   - (b) Earth
   - (c) Venus
   - (d) Neptune

4. I am yellow, cloudy and very hot. Also I am easy to spot. I am being called the evening star. Who am I?
   - (a) Mercury
   - (b) Pluto
   - (c) Mars
   - (d) Venus

5. In which direction Earth revolves around the Sun?
   - (a) East to West
   - (b) West to East
   - (c) North to South
   - (d) South to North

6. When we look at the stars in the sky at night, they differ in brightness. Some are more brighter as compared to others. What could be the most appropriate reason for this variation?
   - (a) It depends on the part of time when we are observing
   - (b) It depends on the amount of light emitted by stars
   - (c) It depends on the distance of star from Earth surface
   - (d) All of the above

7. Consider the following statements about Earth.

   I. Earth takes 24 hours to orbit around the Sun once.

   II. Earth takes 365 days to orbit around the Sun once.

   Choose the correct option.
   - (a) Only I
   - (b) Only II
   - (c) Both I and II
   - (d) Either I or II

8. Which of the following options is the most appropriate reason for changing day and night?
   - (a) Revolution of Earth around Sun
   - (b) Rotation of Earth around Moon
   - (c) Revolution of Earth around Moon
   - (d) Rotation of Earth on its own axis

9. Which of the following arrangements shown in the options below correctly depicts the position of Earth-Moon-Sun during a solar eclipse?

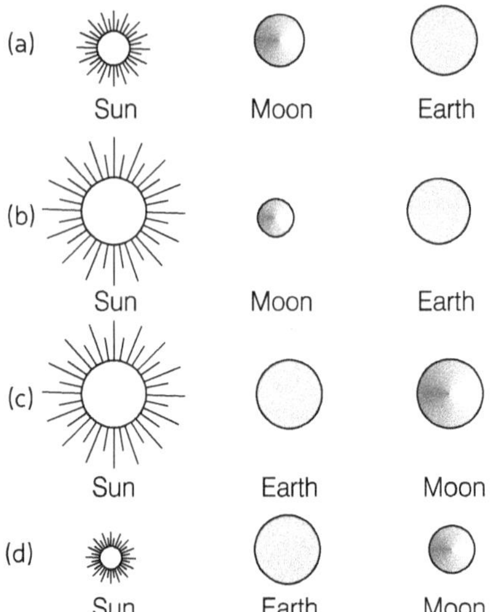

10. Answer in one word by choosing the most appropriate option.

    I. First Indian who travelled in space.

    II. First satellite launched to space.

    III. Vehicle which is used to carry a satellite.

    IV. First astronaut who travelled to space.

    Codes

	I	II	III	IV
(a)	Sunita Williams	Space shuttle	Space ship	Kalpana Chawla
(b)	Kalpana Chawla	Sputnik	Space ship	Sunita Williams
(c)	Yuri Gagarin	Rocket	Sputnik	Rakesh Sharma
(d)	Rakesh Sharma	Sputnik	Rocket	Yuri Gagarin

11. Observe the table given below in which column I represents some planets and column II represents their special character. Choose the one which is incorrectly matched.

	Column I	Column II
(a)	Jupiter	Biggest planet
(b)	Saturn	Beautiful rings
(c)	Earth	Rotates sideways
(d)	Neptune	Coldest planet

12. Consider the following statements about a constellation and choose the correct statement.

    (a) It is a group of stars that are close to Earth

    (b) It is a group of stars that is named after zodiac signs

    (c) It is a group of stars which resembles an unusual animal

    (d) It is a group of stars named for some of recognisable figures seen by astronomers of ancient times

Direction (Q. Nos. 13-15) *Observe the diagram of solar system carefully and answer the questions that follows:*

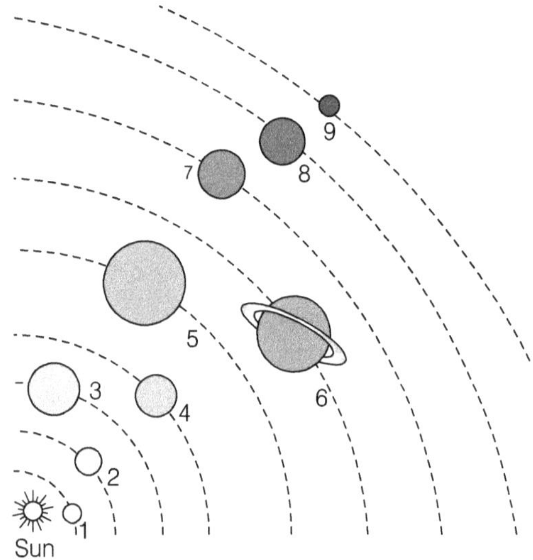

13. Which among them is dwarf planet?

    (a) 8   (b) 9

    (c) Either (a) or (b)   (d) Both (a) and (b)

14. Which of them represents Venus and Jupiter respectively? How many planets are there between them?

    (a) 1, 5; 3   (b) 1, 6; 4

    (c) 2, 5; 2   (d) 2, 6; 3

15. Which of the following options represent the correct sequence of the planets?

	1	2	3	4	5	6	7	8
(a)	Mars	Mercury	Venus	Earth	Uranus	Saturn	Jupiter	Pluto
(b)	Mercury	Earth	Mars	Venus	Saturn	Jupiter	Uranus	Neptune
(c)	Earth	Mars	Mercury	Venus	Jupiter	Uranus	Saturn	Pluto
(d)	Mercury	Venus	Earth	Mars	Jupiter	Saturn	Uranus	Neptune

16. Consider the following statements.
    I. Motion of Earth around the Sun causes variation in seasons.
    II. Motion of Moon around the Earth causes variation in seasons.
    III. Motion of Moon around the Earth causes changes in day and night.
    IV. Motion of Earth around the Sun causes changes in day and night.

Choose the correct option.

(a) I and II (b) II and III
(c) III and IV (d) Only I

17. State true (T) or false (F) using options given below:
    I. Solar system contains milky way galaxy.
    II. Venus is the hottest planet of solar system.
    III. Pluto is the smallest planet of solar system.
    IV. Moon is the natural satellite of a planet.
    V. Group of stars which make some recognisable shape is known as constellation.

Codes

	I	II	III	IV	V
(a)	F	F	T	T	F
(b)	T	F	T	F	F
(c)	F	T	F	T	T
(d)	T	T	F	F	T

18. Complete the following passage using words given in the option below:

Our ......A...... consists of many objects which include Moon, stars, planets and many more. All these objects are known as ......B...... objects. They all revolve around the Sun in predefined ......C...... . Celestial objects can be luminous like ......D...... and non-luminous like ......E...... .

Codes

	A	B	C	D	E
(a)	World	Artificial	Orbits	Moon	Sun
(b)	Universe	Celestial	Orbits	Stars	Planets
(c)	Celestial	Universe	Path	Planets	Stars
(d)	Universe	Celestial	Path	Planets	Moon

19. Fill in the blanks using words given in the options below:
    I. During the ...... Moon day, Moon is not visible.
    II. .... Moon is the small portion of Moon that appears after new Moon.
    III. Complete Moon is visible on ...... Moon day.
    IV. Surface of Moon is not smooth, it contains many .... of different size.
    V. Moon is .... object. It does not have light of its own.

Codes

	I	II	III	IV	V
(a)	New	Crescent	Full	Craters	Non-luminous
(b)	Full	New	Crescent	Holes	Luminous
(c)	Crescent	Full	New	Craters	Non-luminous
(d)	New	Full	Crescent	Holes	Luminous

20. Match the given matrix in context with the nick names of some of the celestial bodies.

A.	Shooting star	(i)	Comets
B.	Morning star	(ii)	Moon
C.	Blue planet	(iii)	Asteroids
D.	Red planet	(iv)	Meteors
E.	Natural satellite	(v)	Mars
		(vi)	Venus
		(vii)	Earth
		(viii)	Sun

Codes

	A	B	C	D	E
(a)	(vi)	(viii)	(i)	(ii)	(iii)
(b)	(i)	(ii)	(iii)	(iv)	(v)
(c)	(iv)	(vi)	(vii)	(v)	(ii)
(d)	(viii)	(vii)	(vi)	(v)	(iv)

Direction (Q. Nos. 21-23) *Read the following information and answer the questions that follows:*

A solar system refers to stars and all the objects that orbit around it. Our solar system consists of Sun, eight planets and their Moons, dwarf planet, asteroids and comets. It resides in an outward spiral of milky way galaxy.

21. Consider the following statements and choose the one which is incorrect in context with the information given above.
   (a) Sun is a star around which all the planets orbit
   (b) Our solar system contains nine planets along with their Moons
   (c) Stars and other objects constitutes a solar system
   (d) Both (b) and (c)

22. In which galaxy, does our solar system exists?
   (a) Spiral galaxy
   (b) Milky way galaxy
   (c) Both (a) and (b)
   (d) Either (a) or (b)

23. In a solar system, Moons orbit around the
   (a) Sun   (b) planets
   (c) asteroids   (d) comets

24. Solve the following crossword using hints given below:

Across

1. Place where astronauts live and work in space.
   (a) Paleontology
   (b) Bunsen burner
   (c) Space station
   (d) Microbiology

3. Planet which is surrounded by bright rings.
   (a) Saturn
   (b) Cosmos
   (c) Fortun
   (d) Volume

5. A person who travels in space.
   (a) Virlogist
   (b) Radiology
   (c) Scientist
   (d) Astronaut

Down

2. Our solar system consists of ...... planets.
   (a) three
   (b) eight
   (c) seven
   (d) datum

4. All the planets revolve around this star in our solar system.
   (a) ram
   (b) dog
   (c) Sun
   (d) chi

6. This planet is also known as morning or evening star.
   (a) Venus
   (b) Earth
   (c) Pluto
   (d) datum

25. What is axis of the Earth?
   (a) It is line passing through Earth
   (b) It is the axis present all around the Earth
   (c) It is an imaginary line that passes straight from North pole to the South pole
   (d) None of the above

26. Which country is known as land of the using Sun?
   (a) USA
   (b) India
   (c) Japan
   (d) Indonesia

CHAPTER 8

Water

1. Which among them is the initial step to treat sewage water to make it fit for drinking?
   (a) Filtration
   (b) Boiling
   (c) Chlorination
   (d) Sedimentation

2. Identify the method shown in figure below to clean water.

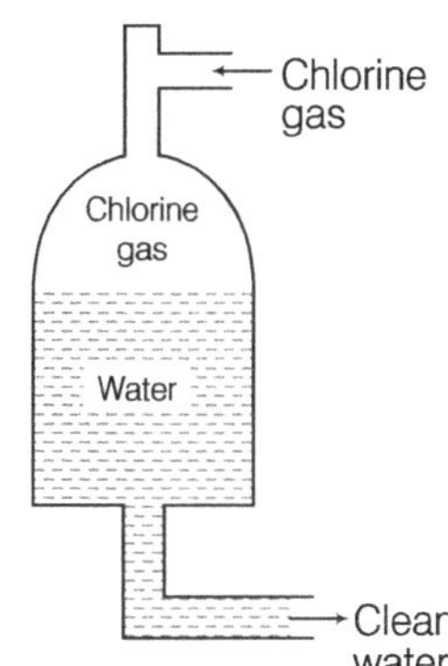

   Codes
   (a) Sedimentation
   (b) Decantation
   (c) Chlorination
   (d) Distillation

3. While purifying water for drinking at home, some steps are used which are listed below. Which of them is not the correct step?
   I. Boiling of water
   II. Filtration of water
   III. Add sugar to water
   IV. Cool the water

   Choose the correct option.
   (a) Only I   (b) Only II   (c) Only III   (d) Only IV

4. Which of the following measures are being taken throughout the country in order to curb uneven distribution of water?
   (a) Building canals
   (b) Rainwater harvesting
   (c) Both (a) and (b)
   (d) Neither (a) nor (b)

5. Given below is a glass filled with icy cool water. When the glass kept in room, some tiny water droplets are formed on the outer surface of glass as shown in the figure.

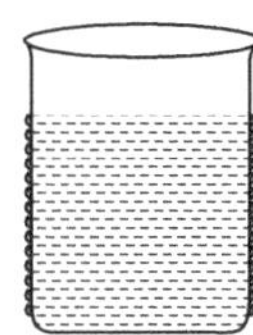

   How does these water droplets deposited around the glass?
   (a) Water in the glass is leaking and deposited around the outer surface of glass
   (b) Water evaporated and get deposited around the outer surface of glass
   (c) Water present in air condenses and get deposited around the outer surface of glass
   (d) Either (a) or (c)

6. Shailey boiled some water in a beaker and covered it using a lid as shown below:

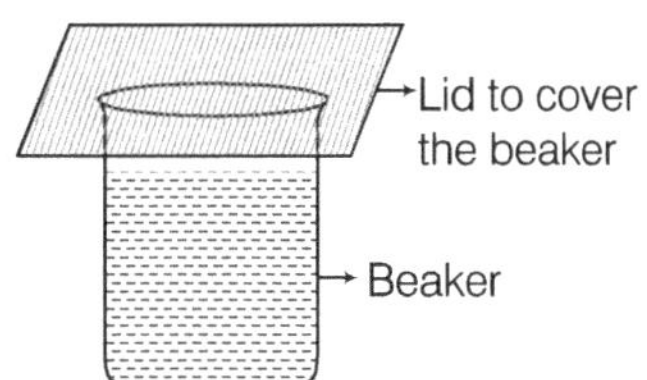

After few minutes, she observed some tiny droplets of water in the inner portion of lid and the empty surface of beaker. She kept the whole system in the freezer as it is for two day. After removing the beaker from the freezer, she tilted it.

Which one of the following diagram depicts the correct observation.

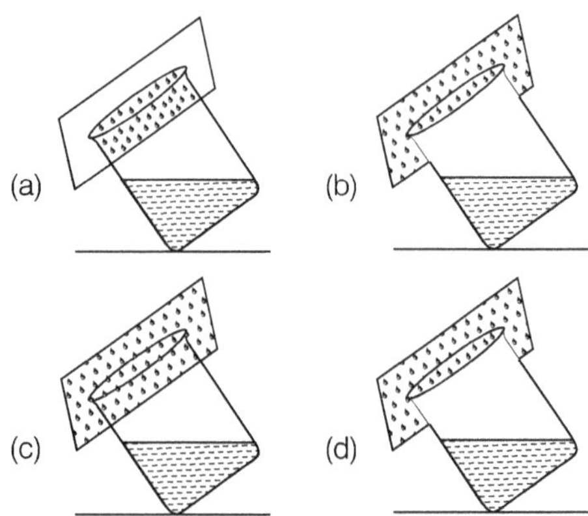

(a)   (b)

(c)   (d)

7. Which of the following method can be employed domestically to make water fit for drinking in less time?

(a) Sedimentation   (b) Filtration
(c) Boiling   (d) Both (a) and (c)

8. Rohit mixed sugar in water and then added sand to it. Which process should he use in order to separate each component?

(a) Boiling and filtration
(b) Filtration and evaporation
(c) Evaporation and condensation
(d) Filtration and condensation

9. Which of these methods can be used to conserve water?

I. Rainwater harvesting.
II. Purification of sewage water.
III. Using water judiciously when required.

Choose the correct option.

(a) I and II   (b) I and III
(c) II and III   (d) All of these

10. A dam is a huge wall with gates built across a river to block the flow of river water. What are the uses of a dam?

I. To make a reservoir.
II. To make canals for irrigation.

III. To generate electricity.
IV. To prevent flood.

Choose the correct option.

(a) I and II   (b) II and III
(c) I and IV   (d) All of these

Direction (Q. Nos. 11-12) *Consider the water cycle shown below carefully and answer the questions that follow:*

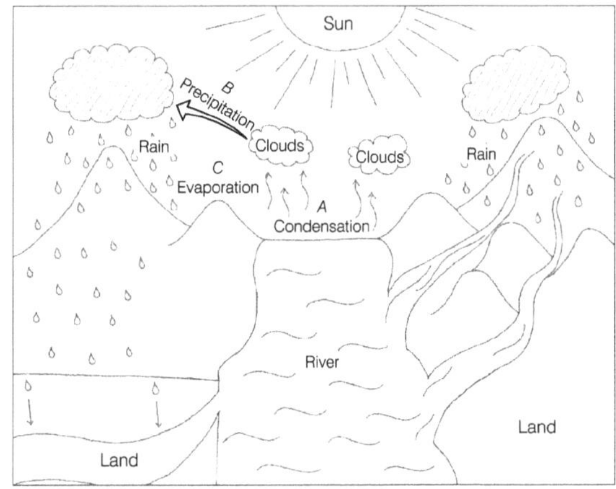

11. Which process in the water cycle shown above is not correctly labelled?

(a) *A*−Condensation   (b) *B*−Precipitation
(c) *C*−Evaporation   (d) All of these

12. What is the need of Sun in a water cycle?

(a) To increase the rate of condensation
(b) To increase the rate of precipitation
(c) To increase the rate of evaporation
(d) To decrease the rate of evaporation

Direction (Q. Nos. 13-14) *Observe the figure shown below carefully and answer the questions that follow:*

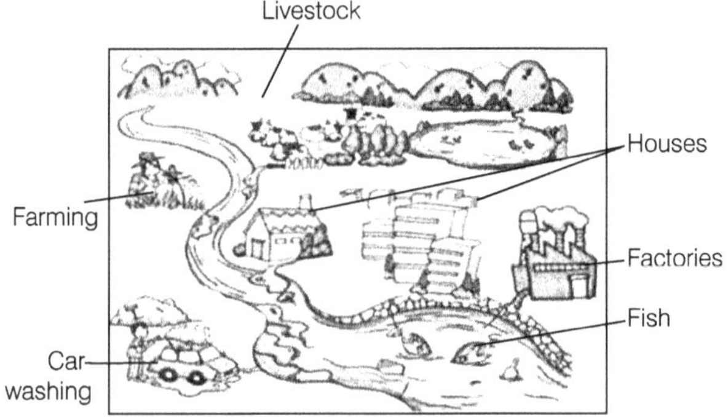

13. How many factors responsible for water pollution are shown in the above figure?

(a) 4   (b) 5

(c) 6   (d) 3

14. What adverse effect of polluting water is depicted in the above figure?

(a) Farming getting terrible

(b) Health of livestock is affected

(c) Life of aquatic animals is in danger

(d) All of the above

15. Consider the set-up shown below in which four blocks A, B, C and D has been placed in a tank filled with water.

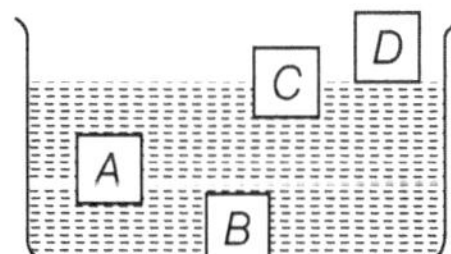

Based on the above experiment, following classification has been made.

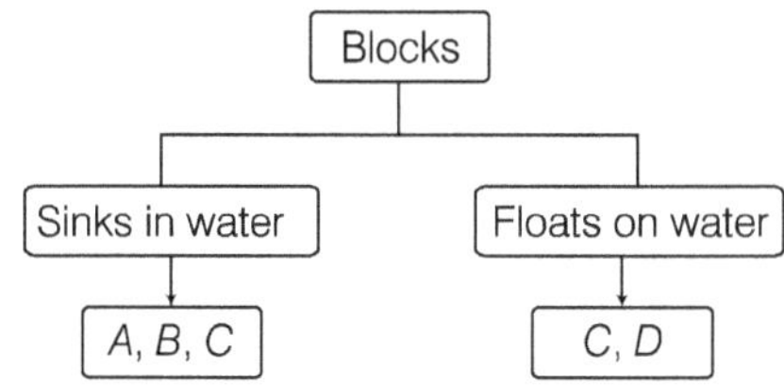

Which of the block is not correctly classified?

(a) A should be in floating group

(b) C should be in sinking group

(c) A and C should be in both the groups

(d) Either (b) or (c)

16. In order to understand the mass and volume concept of water, Rohan took two containers A and B of equal mass. He first filled container A with water upto the brim. Then, he poured all the water in container B without spilling a single drop on ground. The whole set-up is shown below:

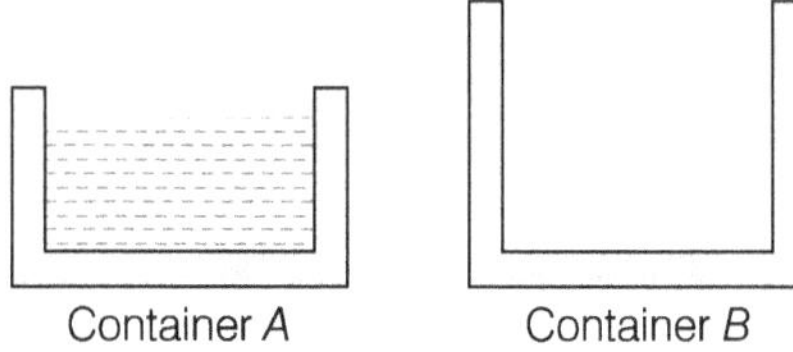

Which of the following is not the correct observation, he will be able to make using above experiment?

(a) The level of water and shape have changed

(b) The volume of water and shape of water have changed

(c) The mass of water and volume of water have changed

(d) The mass of water remain unchanged but shape of water changed

17. Ritu filled four identical beakers A, B, C and D with different substances up to the same level as shown below:

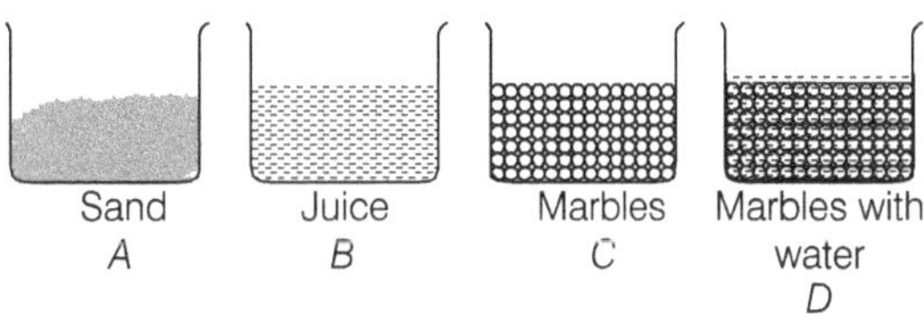

Then she filled each beaker with water up to the brim. Which beaker will require maximum amount of water to get completely filled.

(a) A (b) B

(c) C (d) D

Direction (Q. Nos. 18-19) *Study the flowchart shown below carefully and answer the questions that follow:*

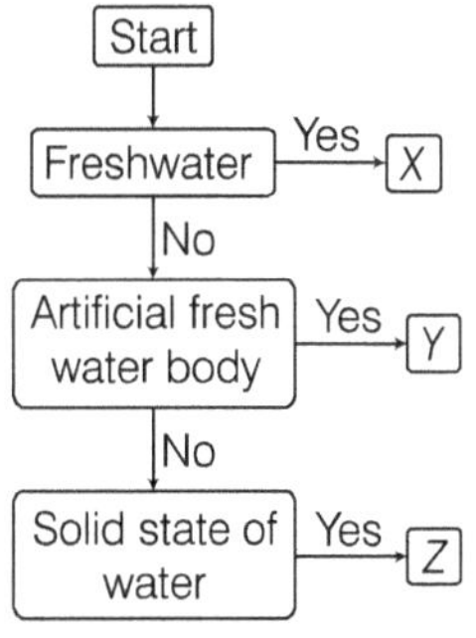

18. Which letter represents clouds?

(a) X (b) Y

(c) Z (d) None of these

19. Reservoirs belongs to which category?

(a) X

(b) Y

(c) Z

(d) Either X or Y

20. During an experiment with water, Riddhi
made a hole at the bottom of a plastic cup
and then inverted it and pushed vertically
downwards in a tub filled with water.

The whole set-up is shown below:

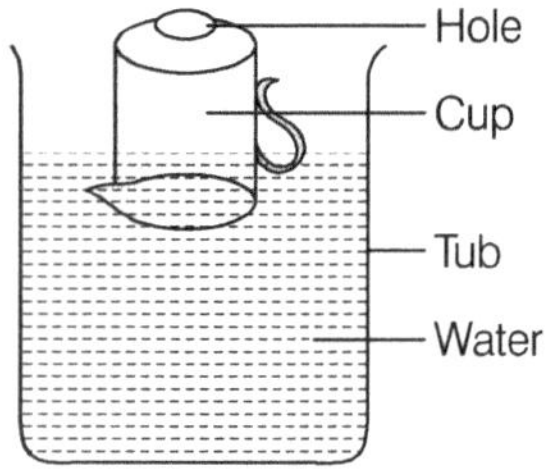

What will happen, when the cup rests at the
bottom of the tub?

(a) Air inside the up escapes out

(b) Level of water in the tub rises

(c) Water fills the cup and overall level remains the
same

(d) Both (a) and (c)

21. Consider the following statements in
context with water pollution.

I. Sewage disposal is the main cause of
water pollution in developing countries.

II. Burning of fossil fuels in large amount
causes water pollution.

III. Water pollution even causes breathing
problems and heart attacks in many
developing countries.

IV. Sewage should be treated before
disposing off in water bodies in order to
curb water pollution.

Choose the correct option.

(a) I and II

(b) II and III

(c) I and III

(d) III and IV

22. Consider the following statements in context
with water.

I. Freshwater is required for irrigation.

II. Rainwater is a source of freshwater.

III. Seawater can be made fit for drinking by
the process of condensation.

Choose the incorrect option.

(a) Only I   (b) Only II

(c) Only III   (d) I and III

23. Complete the passage using words given in
the options below:

Water is an essential component to sustain
......*A*...... on Earth. Earth is covered with ......
B...... of water. But out of this, only ......*C*.......
of water is fresh. The freshwater bodies
include ......*D*...... , rivers and ponds. Sea and
oceans include ....*E*...... water.

Codes

	A	B	C	D	E
(a)	Air	1%	70%	salty	lakes
(b)	Life	70%	1%	lakes	salty
(c)	Fresh	1%	70%	sea	lakes
(d)	Life	70%	1%	sea	river

24. Fill in the blanks using words given in the
options below:

I. During .... , clouds convert into rain
drops.

II. .... involves circulation of water from
oceans to clouds.

III. Use of fertilisers and chemical pesticides
which gets washed into rivers causes
.... pollution.

IV. Water which is suitable for drinking is
known as .... water.

V. The rainwater which seeks into the ground
and collected there is known as ....

Codes

	I	II	III	IV	V
(a)	Evaporation	rain cycle	river	potable	under ground
(b)	Precipitation	water cycle	water	potable	ground water
(c)	Condensation	ground water	air	potable	rain cycle
(d)	Melting	water cycle	water	potable	ground water

25. State true (T) or false (F) using the codes
given below:

I. The level of under ground water in an area
is known as ground water.

II. Water vapours fall as snow when the
atmosphere is extremely cold.

III. Water condenses when heated.

IV. Fresh water is a non-renewable resource.

V. Drinking untreated water can cause
harmful diseases.

	I	II	III	IV	V
(a)	F	T	T	F	T
(b)	T	F	T	F	F
(c)	T	T	F	T	T
(d)	T	T	F	F	F

26. Match the given matrix in context with different forms of water bodies present on Earth.

A.	Large water area surrounded by land	(i)	Reservoir
B.	Hand pumps	(ii)	Ocean
C.	Farmers depend on it to irrigate their fields in India	(iii)	Canal
D.	It covers the largest proportion on earth but not fit to drink	(iv)	Lake
E.	A channel taken out from a river or reservoir	(v)	Rain
		(vi)	Ground water

Codes

	A	B	C	D	E
(a)	(i)	(ii)	(iii)	(iv)	(v)
(b)	(ii)	(i)	(iv)	(iii)	(v)
(c)	(iv)	(vi)	(v)	(ii)	(iii)
(d)	(vi)	(iii)	(i)	(v)	(ii)

Direction (Q. Nos. 27-28) *Read the following information and answer the questions that follow:*

Water cycle is a continuous cycle during which water undergoes various processes including evaporation, condensation and precipitation. During the whole cycle, water keeps on moving and changing from a solid to a liquid to a gas continuously. The process of precipitation helps to fill lakes and rivers and also maintain ground water table.

27. During a water cycle, which process involves formation of rain?
(a) Evaporation   (b) Condensation
(c) Precipitation   (d) Both (b) and (c)

28. Water cycle helps in maintaining ground water table by the process of precipitation. How?

(a) Ground water is absorbed by the process of precipitation
(b) Rainwater is absorbed by the ground which maintains the ground water table
(c) Precipitation involves extraction of ground water to form rain
(d) During precipitation ground water evaporates to form cloud

29. Solve the following crossword using hints given below:

Across

1. Drinking water is also known as ....
(a) polygenic trait   (b) potable water
(c) gravity flow   (d) precipitation

3. This waterbody is used to extract salt by the process of evaporation ....
(a) oceans   (b) marine   (c) deserts   (d) saline

6. An artificial lake being made at the back of a dam by collecting river water.
(a) Reservoir   (b) Water well
(c) Sprinkler   (d) Store well

Down

2. The unwanted material that makes water unfit for drinking.
(a) Reservoir   (b) Snowstorm
(c) Pollutants   (d) Defilement

4. This fresh water body originates from glaciers or springs.
(a) Brooks   (b) Drains   (c) Valley   (d) Rivers

5. The process of converting water into water vapours.
(a) Divining rod   (b) Evaportation
(c) Blizzard   (d) Ice crystals

Work, Force and Energy

1. This simple machine uses a grooved wheel and a rope to carry a load.
   (a) Lever
   (b) Inclined plane
   (c) Wheel and axle
   (d) Pulley

2. This simple machine uses a wheel with a rod joined through its centre which helps in lifting or moving a load?
   (a) Inclined plane
   (b) Wheel and axle
   (c) Screw
   (d) All of these

3. Which of the following is an example of simple machine being used to do work?
   (a) A girl eating a sandwich
   (b) A lady going to second floor of a building using stairs
   (c) A boy runs across a ground
   (d) A shopkeeper counting money

4. This simple machine uses a slanted surface connected from a lower level to a higher level used to carry load through a height.
   (a) Screw
   (b) Wedge
   (c) Lever
   (d) Inclined plane

5. A fork shown in figure below is an example of which type of simple machine?

   (a) Wedge
   (b) Lever
   (c) Screw
   (d) Pulley

6. In which of the following cases pulley can be used?
   (a) To hold pieces of plastic together
   (b) To cut food
   (c) To lift a girder made of iron
   (d) All of the above

7. Which of the following process is not considered as a force?
   (a) Friction   (b) Weight   (c) Gravity   (d) Height

8. Which of the following is (are) example(s) of a pulley system?

   I.    Crane lifting a box

   II.    Elevator

   III.    Well having pulley system

   Codes
   (a) Only I
   (b) Only II
   (c) Only III
   (d) All of these

9. Given below is a loudspeaker. Which energy transformation takes place in a loudspeaker?

      Loudspeaker

(a) Chemical energy → Sound energy
(b) Electrical energy → Sound energy
(c) Light energy → Chemical energy
(d) Sound energy → Electrical energy

10. Consider the figure shown below and identify the parts labelled as *A*, *B* and *C* respectively.

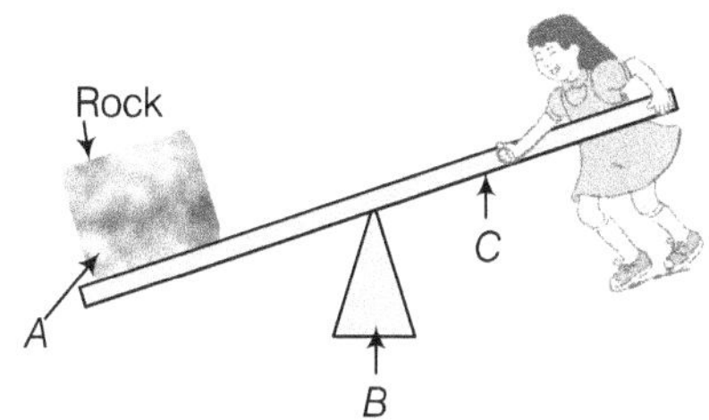

Codes

	A	*B*	*C*
(a)	Lever	Load	Fulcrum
(b)	Load	Fulcrum	Effort
(c)	Load	Lever	Effort
(d)	Object	Wedge	Inclined plane

11. In which of the following examples given below wheel and axle are not used?

   I. Car steering wheel

   II. Door knob

   III. Scissor

Codes
(a) I and II   (b) II and III   (c) Only III   (d) I and III

12. In order to keep a jar at the top most slab of kitchen, Geeta used a wooden staircase as shown in figure below.

Which type of simple machine she used?

(a) Wedge   (b) Staircase
(c) Inclined plane   (d) Either (a) or (b)

13. You are given two blocks of same material and having same mass and dimensions. One is placed on the Earth surface and the other one is sent at Moon. Which of the box will weigh heaviest?
(a) One on the Earth   (b) One on the Moon
(c) Both are equally heavy (d) None of these

14. Consider the following diagrams and choose the one that does not depict a type of lever.

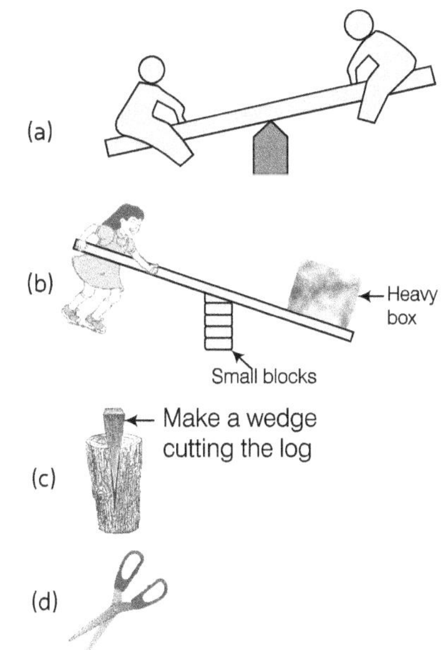

15. Which of the following machines shown below is(are) example(s) of wheel and axle?

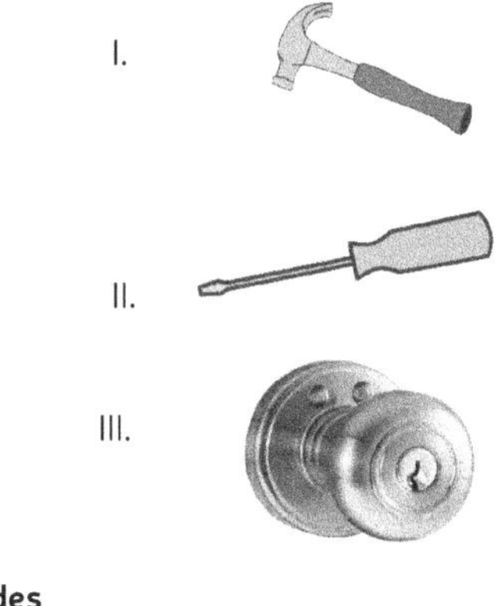

Codes
(a) Only I   (b) Only II
(c) II and III   (d) All of these

16. Given below is a diagram of lever.

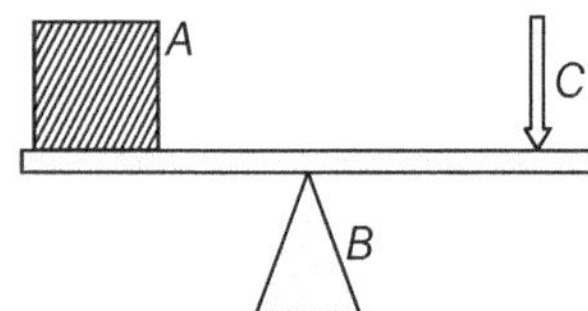

Which object is the same class lever as shown the above?

(a)    (b) 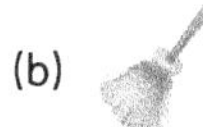

(c)    (d) 

17. Rohit used a pulley shown below to lift a bucket of mass 10 kg.

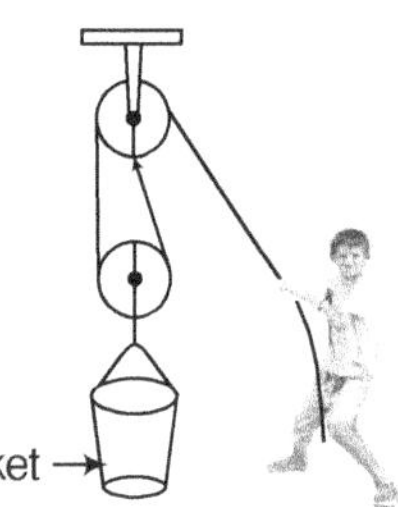

The minimum effort required to lift the bucket will be
(a) 10 kg downwards
(b) 5 kg downwards
(c) 10 kg upwards
(d) 5 kg upwards

18. In order to pull apart a nail from the wall, which of the following simple machine should be used?

(a) 

A lever such as claw ended hammer

(b) 

A wedge such as claw ended hammer

(c) 

A lever such as screw driver
(d) Either of the above

19. In which of the following cases shown below, no work is being done?

I.

Boy pushing the wall

II.

Boy carrying a heavy box

III.

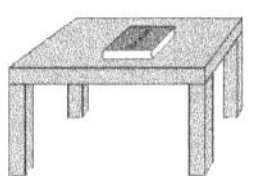

Book lying on table

Codes
(a) Only I   (b) Only II
(c) Only III   (d) All of these

20. Which principle of simple machine is used in a bottle cap shown below?

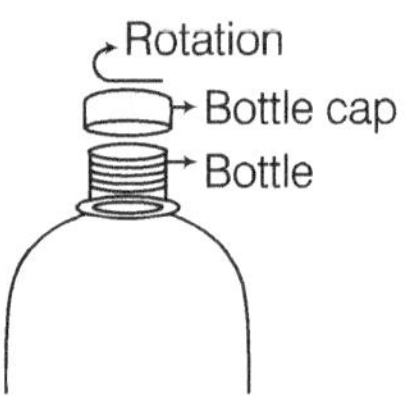

(a) A wedge   (b) Wheel and axle
(c) Screw   (d) Lever

21. Given below is a diagram which shows a kid riding the bicycle. What energy conversion takes place during the ride?

(a) Electrical energy → Kinetic energy
(b) Chemical energy → Potential energy
(c) Electrical energy → Potential energy
(d) Mechanical energy → Kinetic energy

Science Olympiad Class IV

22. Complete the following passage using words given in the options below.

......A...... is also a simple machine. It is basically an ......B...... plane wrapped around a ......C...... . This wrapped inclined plane is known as thread. ......D...... the width of thread be ......E...... force will be required and less time will be taken.

	A	B	C	D	E
(a)	Pulley	Wedge	Inclined	Screw	Sufficient
(b)	Screw	Inclined	Wedge	Narrower	Less
(c)	Machine	Flat	Narrower	Wedge	Less
(d)	Wedge	Screw	Pulley	Machine	More

23. Fill in the blanks using words given in options below.

I. The ability to do work is known as ....

II. A pulley consists of .... and ....

III. Work is done when .... applied on an object moves the object through some distance.

IV. Anything which makes work easier is called ....

V. ..... force is applied to make a machine work.

Codes

	I	II	III	IV	V
(a)	work	rope, wheel	energy	axle	electricity
(b)	energy	wheel, rope	force	machine	muscular
(c)	force	axle, wheel	work	energy	energy
(d)	machine	pulley	pull	force	muscular

24. State true (T) or false (F) using the options given below.

I. The purpose of a simple machine is to make work easier by allowing for a push or pull to occur over an increased distance.

II. The bottom of a light bulb is a screw.

III. A compound machine is two or more simple machines that are working together to make work complicated ....

IV. A see-saw on playground is a wedge ....

V. A pulley opposes the direction of applied force thereby making work easier.

Codes

	I	II	III	IV	V
(a)	F	F	T	T	F
(b)	T	T	F	F	T
(c)	T	F	T	F	T
(d)	F	T	F	T	F

25. Consider the following statements in context with force.

I. A force can change the shape of an object.

II. A force can change the mass of an object.

III. A force can change the direction of a moving object.

Choose the incorrect statement.
(a) Only I
(b) Only II
(c) Only III
(d) All are incorrect

26. Match the given matrix in context with the types of simple machine.

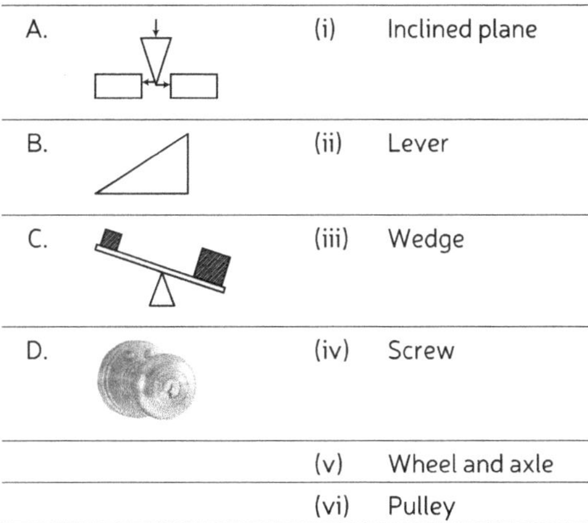

A.		(i)	Inclined plane
B.		(ii)	Lever
C.		(iii)	Wedge
D.		(iv)	Screw
		(v)	Wheel and axle
		(vi)	Pulley

Codes

	A	B	C	D
(a)	(vi)	(v)	(iv)	(i)
(b)	(iii)	(iv)	(i)	(vi)
(c)	(i)	(ii)	(iii)	(iv)
(d)	(iii)	(i)	(ii)	(v)

Force is a push or pull. Even if a boy is sitting idle on chair or a boy running in the garden, force is being applied on both of them. But force applied never confirms work is done. Work can be said to be done only when you apply a force and object moves through a distance.

27. What can you say about work done when a force is applied to a wall?
   (a) Maximum work is done as force applied is maximum
   (b) Minimum work is done as force applied is maximum
   (c) No work is done as wall does not move
   (d) Either (a) or (b)

28. If a force moves an object or changes the direction of motion of an object, what is being done?
   (a) Energy   (b) Power
   (c) Gravity   (d) Work

29. When an object is at rest or does not move, then
   (a) there is just one force acting on the object
   (b) there is no force acting on the object
   (c) there is only stretching force
   (d) there are balanced forces acting on the object

30. Solve the following crossword using hints given below.

Across
2. When you push or pull something you are applying ....
   (a) energy
   (b) force
   (c) flows
   (d) power

4. A scissor consists of two joined together ....
   (a) scale   (b) weigh
   (c) lever   (d) hatch

6. Knife is a .... which used for cutting vegetables.
   (a) slash   (b) wedge
   (c) stick   (d) flake

Down
1. When force applied on an object makes the object move is done ....
   (a) atom   (b) time
   (c) stab   (d) work

3. Sail on a sailboat are raised using this simple machine ....
   (a) volume
   (b) stick
   (c) fossil
   (d) pulley

5. A slide is an example of ....
   (a) rampened plane
   (b) inclined plane
   (c) flatened plane
   (d) flowless plane

Our Environment

1. We are more worried today about pollution because
   I. We have become more cautious.
   II. It has started affecting our lives.
   III. It is a big topic to discuss.
   IV. It is an important criteria to vote for new government.
   Choose the correct option.
   (a) I and II
   (b) I and IV
   (c) III and IV
   (d) II and III

2. Which of the following will not cause water pollution?
   (a) Releasing harmful gases into the air which will cause acid rain
   (b) Using recycled waste water for cleaning
   (c) Putting unwanted waste in abandoned fields
   (d) Throwing chemical waste products into rivers

3. Which of the following statements are correct?
   I. Biodegradable household wastes can increase soil fertility.
   II. Planting of trees can help in preventing soil erosion.
   III. Terrace farming helps in preventing landslides.
   Choose the correct option.
   (a) I and II
   (b) I and III
   (c) I, II and III
   (d) II and III

Direction (Q. Nos. 4 -6) *Observe the given figure and answer the following questions.*

4. What result the given activity will have on the environment?
   (a) Gives out carbon dioxide in the air, so oxygen reduces
   (b) Gives out oxygen in the air, so carbon dioxide reduces
   (c) Gives out nitrogen in the air, so oxygen reduced
   (d) Gives out energy in the air, so gases are reduced

5. The picture is taken during an election rally. The noise produced by the election workers causes the noise pollution.

What will be the effect of this situation?
(a) They are at risk of death
(b) Their ears are affected and become deaf
(c) There will be no effect
(d) They later on enjoy the situation

6. Look at the picture and tell us which type of pollution it is?

(a) Water pollution   (b) Radioactive pollution
(c) Air pollution   (d) Noise pollution

Direction (Q. Nos. 7-9) *Answer the following questions, based on the given passage.*

In Sunderban village, there is beautiful Chikara lake. 5 years ago, it was very clean and had natural plants and different kind of beautiful fishes. But, from the time a chemical factory has been set up there, the lake has started deteriorating and now it just has foul smell and no plants or fishes in it.

7. What may be the reason for such a change in lake?
(a) More washing of clothes of industry workers
(b) Release of pollutants from the industry into water
(c) Increased pollution
(d) Not enough food for fishes

8. Which types of harmful wastes are released by industry?
(a) Hot water and liquid chemical wastes
(b) Soap water
(c) Rainwater
(d) All of the above

9. What should be done to prevent such mishappenings in environment that causes loss of life?
(a) Nothing can be done
(b) More fishes to be put in the lake
(c) Wastes should be first treated and then disposed off in water
(d) Industry should be shut down

10. Soil supports life; both plants and animals. Which of the following can cause pollution of soil?
(a) Chemicals like dyes leaked in soil
(b) Excess fertiliser use in soil
(c) Garbage dumped into holes dug up in soil
(d) All of the above

11. What effect does pollution has on the soil?
    I. Reduces the quality of soil.
    II. Soil becomes inefficient to support life.
    III. Soil can become poisonous.
    IV. Large number of plants can grow on soil.

Choose the correct option.
(a) I, II and III   (b) I, III and IV
(c) II, III and IV   (d) I, II and IV

12. Classify the following sources of pollution into three classes based on which type of pollution do they cause?

> Burning of fuels, Soil Erosion, Landfills, Mining, Fertilisers, Automobiles

	Air pollution	Soil pollution	Water pollution
(a)	Burning of fuels, automobiles	Landfills, mining	Fertilisers, soil erosion
(b)	Burning of fuels, soil erosion	Fertilisers, mining	Landfills, automobiles
(c)	Mining, fertilisers	Landfills, Soil erosion	Burning of fuels, automobiles
(d)	Landfills, automobiles	Burning of fuels, soil erosion	Mining, fertilisers

Direction (Q. Nos. 13-15) *"Earth is a much warmer place than it should be. This is due to air pollution".*

13. Which of the following pollutant may be responsible for such increase in temperature of earth?
(a) Oxygen   (b) Carbon dioxide
(c) Hydrogen   (d) Nitrogen

14. What is this phenomenon of increase in Earth's temperature known as?
(a) Global warming
(b) Earth's warming
(c) Sun's trapping
(d) Light house effect

15. How does Earth's temperature increase due to increase in concentration of pollutant?
 (a) They trap Sun's heat and does not allow it to escape
 (b) They themselves emit heat
 (c) They cause forest fires and thus heat up the atmosphere
 (d) All of the above

16. Greenhouse effect and global warming affect the environment and peoples' life too. Arrange following incidences in correct order.
 I. Loss of property and life and less land for growing population to live.
 II. Rise in temperature causes melting ice of North and South poles.
 III. Lower and coastal areas may get flood.
 IV. Temperature of Earth rises.
 Codes
 (a) IV → II → III → I   (b) IV → I → III → II
 (c) IV → I → II → III   (d) I → IV → II → III

17. What from the following is unexpected weather changes due to rise in pollution?
 (a) Snowfall in Saudi Arabia
 (b) Widespread floods in Europe
 (c) Very heavy snowfall in Kashmir
 (d) All of the above

18. Match the following columns.

A.	Ozone	(i)	Harms surfaces of buildings and soil
B.	Acid rain	(ii)	Rise in temperature of Earth
C.	Pollution	(iii)	Protects from harmful ultraviolet rays of the Sun
D.	Greenhouse effect	(iv)	Contamination of the environment with harmful substances

Codes

	A	B	C	D		A	B	C	D
(a)	(i)	(iii)	(ii)	(iv)	(b)	(i)	(ii)	(iii)	(iv)
(c)	(iii)	(i)	(iv)	(ii)	(d)	(iv)	(ii)	(iii)	(i)

19. Rearrange different steps of occurrence of acid rain in correct order;
 I. Mixes with water vapours in the air and come down with rain.
 II. Acid rain is the result.
 III. Gases remain in the air.
 IV. Burning of fuel releases harmful gases.
 Codes
 (a) IV → III → I → II
 (b) I → III → II → IV
 (c) II → IV → III → I
 (d) I → III → IV → II

20. Read the following statements.
 I. We can control pollution within few days.
 II. Factories should use filters that clean the air before released in atmosphere.
 III. CNG should be used in the vehicles.
 IV. Air pollutants like dust and dust particles may reduce vision.

 Choose the correct option.

	I	II	III	IV
(a)	F	T	F	T
(b)	F	F	T	T
(c)	T	F	F	F
(d)	F	T	T	T

21. The waste we produce can be divided into two types, biodegradable and non-biodegradable wastes. Arrange following wastes in two categories mentioned above.

> Vegetable peel, Plastic, Books, Glass, Thermacol, Human excreta, Metals

	Biodegradable wastes	Non-biodegradable wastes
(a)	Vegetable peel, books, human excreta	Plastic, glass, metals, thermacol
(b)	Plastic, books, metals	Vegetable peel, glass, human excreta
(c)	Glass, thermacol, books	Human excreta, metals, plastic
(d)	Vegetable peel, glass, human excreta	Plastic, thermacol, books

22. Teacher asked the Sia about the bad effects of pollution. She gave few points. Did she gave all correct answers?
 Statement A Surroundings look dirty and ugly.
 Statement B Diseases like diarrhoea, dysentry, typhoid may spread.
 Statement C It gives out fowl smell.

(a) Statement A is correct, but Statement B and C are wrong
(b) Statement A and C are correct, but Statement B is wrong
(c) Statement B and C are correct, but Statement A is wrong
(d) All the statements are correct

23. Match the following columns.

A.	Burning	(i)	Garbage dumped in the open, away from a town or city
B.	Composting	(ii)	Garbage dumped in the deep ditches which are dug in the ground
C.	Landfills	(iii)	Garbage is collected and burnt
D.	Open dumping	(iv)	Degradable waste dumped into a pit to convert into manure

Codes

	A	B	C	D		A	B	C	D
(a)	(i)	(iii)	(ii)	(iv)	(b)	(ii)	(iii)	(iv)	(i)
(c)	(iii)	(iv)	(ii)	(i)	(d)	(iv)	(ii)	(iii)	(i)

24. Why does 'Kabari wala' buy old newspapers and magazines from us?
(a) They resell them in the villages and earn money
(b) They sell it to the factories which make fresh paper from the old papers
(c) They burn them to warm up the cold areas
(d) They make envelopes from them

25. What are the 3 R's to keep the environment clean?
(a) Reuse, reduse, retreat
(b) Reuse, reduce, recycle
(c) Repair, reuse, reduce
(d) Recreate, reform, recycle

26. Air is a mixture of gases that supports life on Earth. Which of the following gives correct composition of the air?

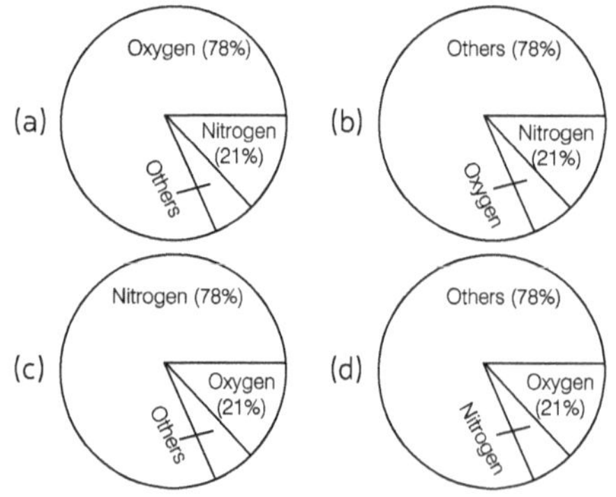

27. One hot summer day, Veer planned to go out with his family in his car, which was parked outside in the Sun. When they opened and sat in the car, they found it to be extremely hot, even more than the outside. What may be the reason?
(a) AC of the car was not working
(b) Car became a greenhouse. The glasses of the car didn't allow the Sun's heat to escape and thus temperature increased
(c) As the car was closed, so there was no cool air inside the car
(d) Car is made up of metal, so it became hot

28. Solve the following crossword using hints given below:

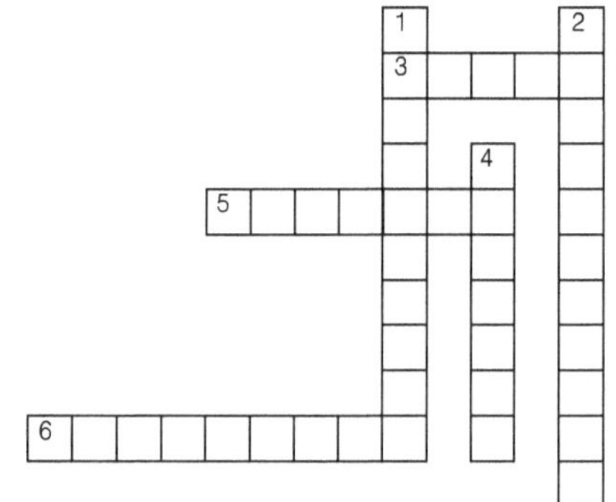

Across

3. .... is thin layer of invisible gas in the upper atmosphere.
(a) Ozone (b) Salal (c) Argon (d) aryne

5. We should .... off the garbage properly.
(a) recycle (b) dispose (c) dumping (d) burning

6. Air pollution can lead to reduce vision and also .... difficulties.
(a) designing (b) breathing
(c) digestion (d) smellting

Down

1. By.........., we convert wastes into manure.
(a) washing (b) converting
(c) retreating (d) composting

2. Excess use of .... causes water pollution.
(a) polythenes (b) seeds
(c) fertilisers (d) irrigation

4. If we are making pencil holders from aluminium canes or plastic jars, what are we doing?
(a) Dispose (b) Reusing (c) Cycling (d) Distend

Practice Set 1

A Test Based on the Whole Content of Class 4th

1. Which of the following is wrongly matched with their group?

(a) Ants–Colony   (b) Cows–Herd
(c) Owl–Parliament   (d) Deer–Pride

2. Given below is the life cycle of cockroach. Some parts are missed out to be labelled. Label them, so as to complete the diagram.

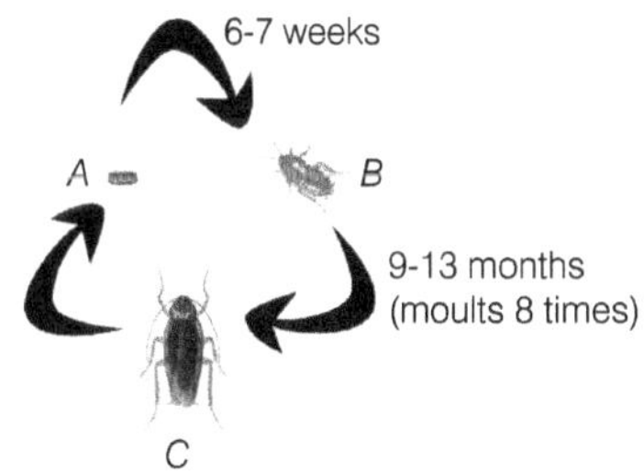

Codes

	A	B	C
(a)	Eggs	Nymph	Adult
(b)	Nymph	Eggs	Adult
(c)	Adult	Nymph	Eggs
(d)	Eggs	Adult	Nymph

3. If we do not take care of our mouth, we can get even toothache. Arrange following steps causing toothache in correct sequence.

  I. Acid creates cavity in teeth causing toothache.
  II. Bits of food sticks to the tooth.
  III. Germs salt (bacteria) grow in the mouth.
  IV. Germs breakdown the food particles which produces acid.

Codes

(a) II, III, IV, I   (b) I, IV, III, II
(c) II, IV, III, I   (d) IV, II, III, I

4. As we all know that digestion of food begins in mouth itself. Match correctly the different processes that take place in mouth to aid digestion.

A. Teeth   (i) Softens the food to a pulp.
B. Saliva   (ii) Pushes bits of food to food pipe.
C. Tongue   (iii) Break up the food into smaller particles.

Codes

	A	B	C
(a)	(iii)	(ii)	(i)
(b)	(i)	(iii)	(ii)
(c)	(i)	(ii)	(iii)
(d)	(ii)	(i)	(iii)

Direction (Q.Nos. 5-6) *Carefully study the diagram drawn by Keshav and answer the following questions.*

'Keshav studied photosynthesis process in the class and drew the diagram, but he missed out labelling few components'.

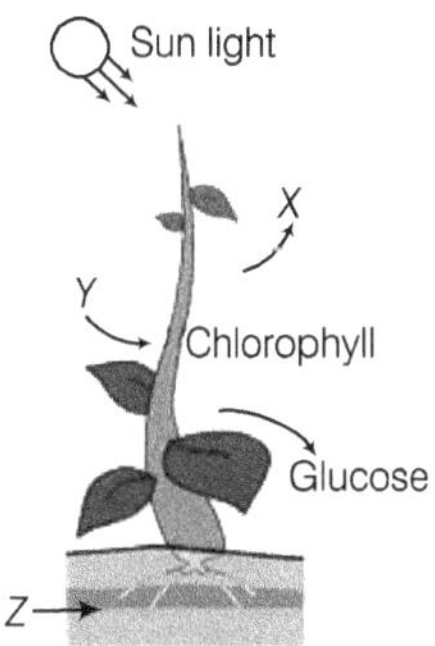

5. What does the arrow Z represent?
(a) Release of water and minerals to the soil
(b) Absorption of water and minerals from the soil by roots
(c) Absorption of carbon dioxide from soil
(d) Release of oxygen into the atmosphere

6. Absorption of carbon dioxide and release of oxygen is represented by which arrow?
(a) X and Y
(b) Y and X
(c) Y and Z
(d) Z and X

7. Weight of an object on Moon is 1/6 of the Earth. Does mass of an object also be different on Moon with respect to Earth?
(a) Yes, because it also depends on the gravity
(b) No, because Earth and Moon are of same size
(c) Yes, because weight and mass are same for an object
(d) No, because it does not depend on the gravity

8. Match the following animals with their shelters.

A. Earthworm   (i) Stable
B. *Hippopotamus*   (ii) Nest on tree
C. Horses   (iii) Under the ground
D. Woodpecker   (iv) Land and water

Codes

	A	B	C	D
(a)	(i)	(ii)	(iii)	(iv)
(b)	(ii)	(iii)	(iv)	(i)
(c)	(iii)	(iv)	(i)	(ii)
(d)	(iv)	(i)	(ii)	(iii)

9. Read the following statements and choose the correct option.

  I. In big cities and towns, people live in pucca houses.
  II. Kuchcha houses of villages do not need to be repaired often.
  III. Dharavi in Mumbai is one of the largest slum in Asia.
  IV. Multistoreyed building is an ideal breeding ground for mosquitoes and flies.

Codes

	I	II	III	IV
(a)	T	T	F	F
(b)	F	F	T	T
(c)	T	F	T	F
(d)	F	T	F	T

10. Look at the picture and predict the best use of this biodegradable dried leaves?

Dried leaves

(a) Burnt these leaves
(b) Leaves can be used to make manure
(c) Leaves can be thrown in open air
(d) Leaves are useless

11. Read the following statements and choose correct option based on these statements.
Statement A Satellites are used to know about the weather.
Statement B Satellites are used to know the area of land and water.
Statement C Satellites are used for distant communication.
(a) Statements A and B are correct, statement C is incorrect
(b) All statements are correct
(c) Statements A and C are correct; statement B is incorrect
(d) Statements B and C are correct; statement A is incorrect

12. When we burn incense sticks in one corner of the house, we can smell it easily in all other corners of the house. What is responsible for this?
(a) Gases flow easily and fill the entire space available, so taking smell of incense stick in all the corners of house
(b) Water vapours in the atmosphere moves and takes the smell of incense sticks in all the corners of the room
(c) Because we carry the incense sticks to all the corners of the house
(d) All of the above

Direction (Q.Nos. 13-14) *We have two sets of teeth during our lifetime. One is milk teeth and the other is permanent teeth.*

13. What is the number of milk teeth and permanent teeth in humans?
(a) Milk:20   Permanent:32
(b) Milk:32   Permanent:20
(c) Milk:16   Permanent:10
(d) Milk:15   Permanent:25

14. Out of these two, one is replaced by the other. Choose the correct option.
(a) Milk teeth falls and are replaced by permanent teeth
(b) It depends on person to person
(c) Permanent teeth falls and are replaced by milk teeth
(d) Both falls and are replaced by deciduous teeth

15. Solve the following crossword using hints given below:

Across

1. Appearance of water droplets outside a glass of cold water is an example of
(a) evaporation   (b) condensation
(c) contractions   (d) presentation

3. It is the process in which a solid turns into a liquid on heating.
(a) Lenient
(b) Thawing
(c) Melting
(d) Climent

4. ....is when a cup of water when placed in a colder region, turns into hard ice.
(a) Freezing
(b) Soliding
(c) Cemented
(d) Moulding

Down

2. Process of change of liquid into gas on heating.
(a) Evaporation
(b) Contraction
(c) Indigestion
(d) Shrinkation

Practice Set 2

A Test Based on the Whole Content of Class 4th

1. Both mosquito and butterfly are insects and both have a four stage life-cycle. Then, what is the difference between their egg laying habits ?
   (a) Butterfly lay eggs on surface of still water, whereas mosquitoes lay eggs under leaves of plants
   (b) Butterfly lay eggs under leaves of plants, whereas mosquitoes lay eggs on surface of still water
   (c) Butterfly lay many eggs, whereas mosquitoes lay 1-2 eggs at one time
   (d) Butterfly eggs are much bigger than eggs of mosquitoes

2. An adult frog can breathe through its ...A... in water and with its ...B... on land. It has long hind legs that help it ...C... on land and ...D... feet that help it to swim in water.
   Codes

	A	B	C	D
(a)	Gills	Lungs	Crawl	Broad
(b)	Moist skin	Lungs	Move	Flat
(c)	Moist skin	Lungs	Hop	Webbed
(d)	Dry skin	Gills	Sleep	Flipper

3.  : ...A... help you to bite the food.

 : ...B... help you to tear the food.

: ...C... help you to grind the food.

: ...D... help you to crack the food.

Codes

	A	B	C	D
(a)	Premolar	Molar	Incisor	Canine
(b)	Canine	Premolar	Molar	Incisor
(c)	Incisor	Canine	Premolar	Molar
(d)	Molar	Incisor	Canine	Premolar

4. Which part of the following do we consume;

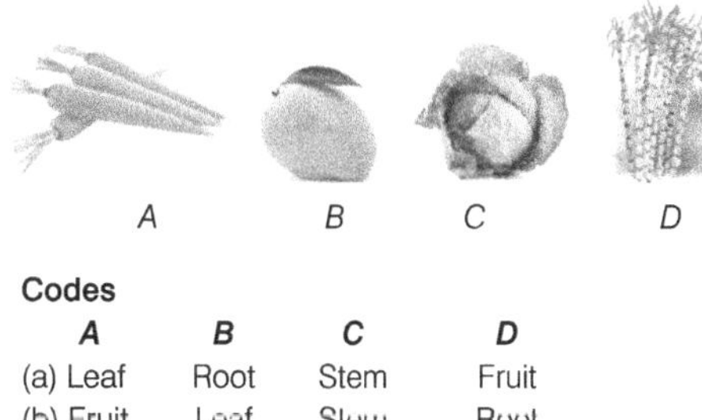

A   B   C   D

Codes

	A	B	C	D
(a)	Leaf	Root	Stem	Fruit
(b)	Fruit	Leaf	Stem	Root
(c)	Root	Fruit	Leaf	Stem
(d)	Fruit	Stem	Root	Leaf

5. Match the following columns.

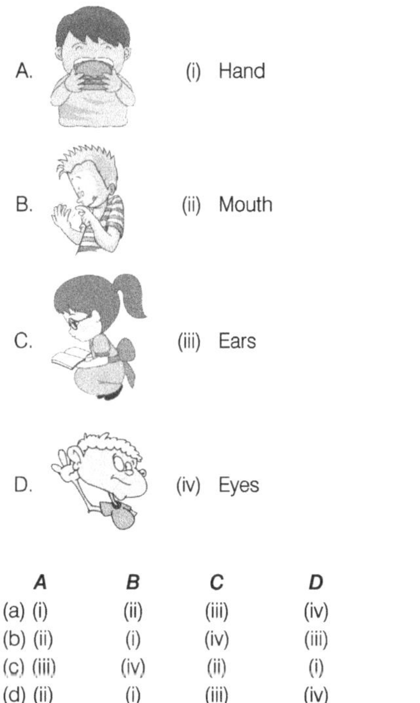

A.	(i) Hand
B.	(ii) Mouth
C.	(iii) Ears
D.	(iv) Eyes

	A	B	C	D
(a)	(i)	(ii)	(iii)	(iv)
(b)	(ii)	(i)	(iv)	(iii)
(c)	(iii)	(iv)	(ii)	(i)
(d)	(ii)	(i)	(iii)	(iv)

Direction (Q.No. 6) *Read the following passage and answer following questions that follow:*

" Moon has less gravitational force than Earth. The gravity of Moon is 1/6 of the Earth and so, we weigh 6 times less on the Moon than on Earth".

6. If a person weighs 72 kg on Earth, what will be his weight on Moon?
(a) 12 kg
(b) 18 kg
(c) 36 kg
(d) 9 kg

7. Match the following pictures of means of transport with their utility.

A. 
(i) Used in deserts to carry goods and people.

B. 
(ii) Used in mountains to carry goods and people.

C. 
(iii) Used by kings to pull their chariots.

D. 
(iv) Used to carry goods and people.

Codes

	A	B	C	D
(a)	(i)	(iii)	(ii)	(iv)
(b)	(iv)	(iii)	(ii)	(i)
(c)	(iii)	(i)	(iv)	(ii)
(d)	(iv)	(ii)	(iii)	(i)

8. Complete the following diagram of solar system.

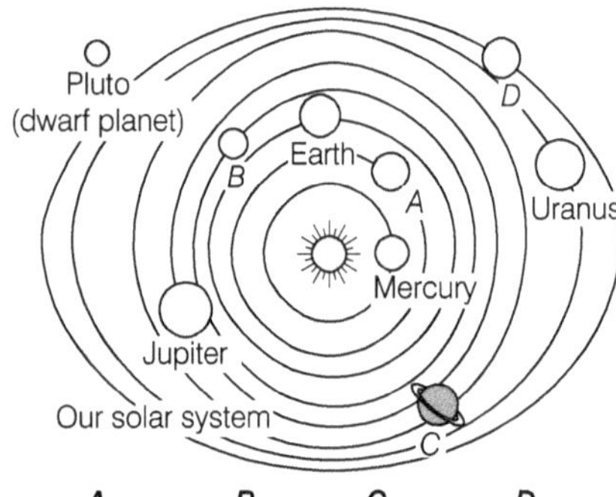

	A	B	C	D
(a)	Saturn	Neptune	Venus	Mars
(b)	Mars	Saturn	Neptune	Venus
(c)	Venus	Mars	Saturn	Neptune
(d)	Neptune	Venus	Mars	Saturn

9. 'Rotation is movement of a planet around its central axis. Earth rotates once upon its axis in ...A... whereas Neptune takes only ...B... to rotate once. Planet ...C... takes same time to rotate once as the Earth'.

	A	B	C
(a)	24 hours	15 hours	Mars
(b)	18 hours	12 hours	Venus
(c)	15 hours	24 hours	Venus
(d)	12 hours	18 hours	Mars

10. Given are different steps of an activity of making salt from salt water(sea water) in laboratory. Arrange them in correct sequence.
I. Boil it until the water evaporates.
II. Pour this salt water into a pan.
III. This white powder is actually salt.
IV. Dissolve 4 tablespoon of salt in a glass of water.
V. A layer of white powder forms at the bottom of the pan.
(a) I, II, IV, III, V
(b) V, III, I, II, IV
(c) IV, II, I, III, V
(d) II, III, IV, IV

11. Which of the following is paired wrongly?
(a) Dam – Water storage
(b) Rainfed ocean – Brahmaputra
(c) Tubewell – Underground water
(d) River – Ganga

12. Match the following columns.

A. Water	(i) Physical change
B. Sugar	(ii) Solute
C. Burning of candle	(iii) Solvent
D. Slicing of bread	(iv) Chemical change

Codes

	A	B	C	D
(a)	(i)	(ii)	(iii)	(iv)
(b)	(ii)	(iii)	(iv)	(i)
(c)	(iii)	(ii)	(iv)	(i)
(d)	(iv)	(i)	(ii)	(iii)

13. Which of the following is not correctly paired?
(a) Lungs – Carbon dioxide
(b) Kidney – Body waste
(c) Immune system – Diseases
(d) Brain – Digestion

14. "Taj Mahal in Agra is made up of white marble. But few years back, it started turning yellow and thus became a matter of concern for the government".

What do you think was the reason behind Taj Mahal turning yellow?
(a) Due to chemicals given out by the factories near it
(b) Due to white marble getting old
(c) It was actually yellow marble polished white and now white colour has been washed away
(d) Due to too many tourists visiting the place

Answers *and* Explanations

① Matter

1. **(c)** Matter is anything which occupies space. Shadow is formed when an object comes in contact with light. It is an image. Heat from the sun is a form of energy (light energy). It does not occupy space. Hence, both A and C are not matter. Clouds have mass because the water in it occupies the space. Rain is a form of water and is liquid in nature. It is a form of matter.

2. **(b)** Matter A is a liquid because it cannot be compressed and does not have definite shape. Matter B is a gas because it does not have definite shape and definite volume and it can also be compressed easily. Matter C is a said because it has a definite shape and a definite volume. It cannot be compressed easily.

3. **(d)** Option 'd' has correct property and state. Salt particles are solid in nature and they have definite shape. Milk is a liquid. So, it does not have definite volume similarly, shampoo is also a liquid. Oxygen is a gas, it does not have definite shape and volume both.

4. **(d)** Only shape and volume has changed. The clay is a object which has a mass and hence called as matter. This is the fundamental property of matter. So, mass remains unchanged.

5. **(d)** Snow, toothbrush and dust are matter because they occupies space and have mass. While light, heat and sound are the form of energies. They do not have mass and hence, are called as non-matter.

6. **(c)** Both group A and group B materials are two different states of matter and both possess mass too. Hence, option (c) is the correct answer.

7. **(d)** The set-up confirms that gases have mass. When balloon B got punchured, the air which a mass comes out. As a result, the weight of balloon B decreases and a disbalance is observed.

8. **(b)** Material 'B' is most suitable material to make raincoat. The essential condition for raincoat is being waterproof and flexible. Although, it easily breaks when dropped from a height. It can be considered a good material.

9. **(a)** The shape of P was not affected when wedge was removed so, P is a solid. Q must be liquid because it changed its shape accordingly and not a gas because the beaker is open and gas would have escaped out of open beaker. Hence, option (a) is the correct answer.

10. **(b)** All the bags weigh 1kg which means they have same mass. The volume of all the bags is different because they all are different materials. Hence, option (b) is the correct answer.

11. **(a)** Since, the opening of syringe is closed by the finger so, water and air will not get any extra space to escape out because of which no change in volume is seen. Hence, option (a) is the correct answer.

12. **(a)** Snow flakes are the solid form of water. They are solid in nature. They have mass. They have definite shape and definite volume.

13. **(c)** Matter C does not have fixed volume. The matter which does not have fixed volume are gases. They are highly compressible. Hence, option (c) is correct.

14. **(a)** Oil and milk are liquid in nature. They both do not have fixed shape and can easily flow.

15. **(d)** B is not affected by plastic. Anything which is not affected by the other thing is more harder and stronger. Hence, B is harder than plastic.

16. **(b)** The material required for a book shelf should be highly rigid and strong. Hence, option (b) is the correct answer.

17. **(d)** At room temperature, when beaker gets tilted it does not change it shape and hence, found to be solid. But when the beaker was heated, it changes its shape and have flowing property. Which suggests that now it is a liquid

18. **(b)** Since, all the three cylinders are made up of different materials, so their mass is different. They all have equal volume of $100\,cm^3$. Hence, option (b) is the correct answer.

19. **(a)** A has the highest mass. A is heavier than B and D while D is only heavier than C. So, it is concluded that A is heaviest and has highest mass.

20. *X* should be a heat resistant material. Material
(b) which does not get heated. So, that a person can easily picked the hot pan. While *Y* should be made up of heat conducting material which can easily warm the contents of frying pan. Hence, option (b) is the correct answer.

21. Since, spring balance made up of material *X*
(b) holded the block firmly whereas, spring balance made up of material *Y* broke down. It shows material *X* is stronger than material *Y*. Hence, option (b) is the correct answer.

22. Liquid *A* and *B* have same mass. Because both
(a) the containers are balanced on lever. A lever is a machine which can be used for weighing the substances. The liquid *A* and *B* both have equal mass but different volumes liquid *B* has smaller volume than liquid *A*.

23. Everything which exist on Earth can be grouped
(d) into three states of matter. These are solid, liquid or gas. The general properties that we look in a matter are its mass, volume and shape.

24. I. **Atom** is the smallest part of matter.
(b) II. The molecules of **liquid** are loosely packed compared to solids and tightly packed compared to **gas**.
III. Volume is the amount of **space** a matter occupies.
IV. Matter has **mass**.

25. I. Liquids cannot be held freely in hand. They do
(c) not have definite shape. They can easily flow. When, they are taken on hand, it can easily flow out from hand.
II. Solid moth balls directly convert into gas using sublimation. This statement is true. Sublimation is a process in which solid substance directly converted into gas on exposure with that.
III. The molecules of solid are tightly packed with each other. This is reason for solids rigidity. The force attraction between the molecules is maximum.
IV. Solids have definite shape and mass.
V. A molecule is formed when two or more atoms join together.

26. A. Milk ⟶ icecream   (v) Freezing
(d) B. Clouds ⟶ raindrops   (iii) Precipitation
C. Water vapours ⟶ clouds (ii) Condensation
D. Ice ⟶ water   (iv) Melting

27. Water when freezes, converts into ice which is
(b) solid form of water. Hence, option (b) is the correct answer.

28. Ice is solid and has fixed shape and volume.
(c) Water is liquid and has only definite volume. Water vapours are gases and has neither definite shape nor definite volume. Hence, option (c) is the correct answer.

29. **Across**
1. The amount of space occupied by a matter–
(a) Volume.

3. The tiny particles that join to make up a matter–
(c) Atom.

7. Water in the form of gas is– Water vapour.
(a)

8. Solid white flakes of water that fall from the sky
(c) are known as– Snow.

Down
2. Raindrops are in the state of– Liquid.
(b)

4. The amount of matter contained is– Mass
(b)

5. When atoms are in this state, they fly around
(b) freely– Gas.

6. They process in which liquid water turns into
(a) gas– Evaporation.

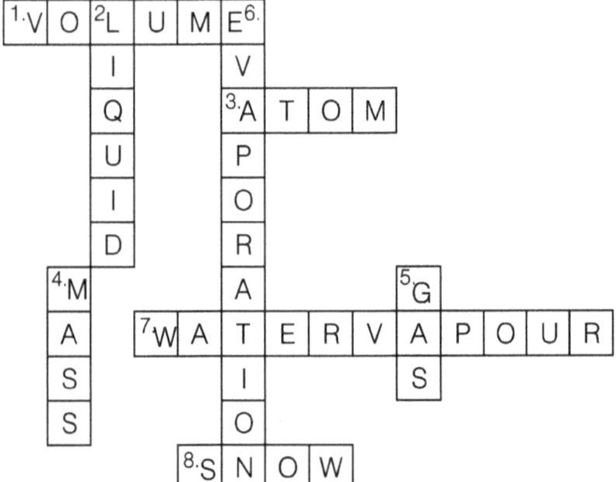

(2) Animals

1. *(a)* Group of elephants is called herd. Group of lions is called pride. Group of monkeys is called band and group of fishes is called school.

2. *(a)* Migratory birds fly in 'V' formation which reduce air resistance, allowing them to conserve their energy. Air resistance is the forces that are in opposition to the relative motion of an object through the air. When air resistance reduces, it is for birds to fly easily and smoothly.

3. *(d)* Shy animals are those animals which loves to live with their own species. They generally don't indulge with the other species and are not interactive, e.g. squirrel, deer, bear, monkey.

Friendly animals are those animals which love to move around, interact with other species, e.g. dog, cow, hen, dolphins.

4. *(b)* Bears have black skin colour. As black colour can absorb maximum light so, black skin colour absorbs more light to keep their body warm. So, the option (b) is incorrect.

5. *(a)* Tiger and sparrow have correct characteristics. Tigers have hairs on the body. They do not have scales. They have two types of ears external and internal ears. Sparrow have hairs on the body. They have feathers. They have internal ears.

Fish does not have hair on the body. They have scales. They do not have ears, instead they have holes.
Snake does not have hair on the body. They have scales. Snakes do not have ears, they can't hear.

6. *(c)* Birds riding on cows/buffaloes are called cattle egrets and those riding on giraffe/oxen are called ox peckers. These birds get food from these animals. They feed on the insects which, host on the body of cows.

7. *(b)* Birds get their food as they eat insects, which lie in the skin of these animals. This is a type of mutual interaction.

8. *(c)* Elephants have big ears, *Hippopotamus* have small ears, birds have small hole on sides of their head and snakes don't have ears.

9. *(a)* Fishes and snakes do not have hairs on their bodies rather they have scales on their bodies. These scales help in the respiration process. Cow, goat and tiger are mammals and they have hair on their bodies. These hairs are used to warm their bodies and also for protection.

10. *(b)* A – Egg shell, B – Yolk, C – Albumin

Egg shell is the outer covering of the egg. It protects the egg from hard conditions.

Yolk is the premature condition of the babyhen (chick). It is rich is fat.

Albumin is the colourless fluid present around the yolk. It is rich in protein.

11. *(c)* Parent bird lays eggs. Parent bird sits on the egg to keep it warm. Embryo develops into chick and chick breaks the shell and comes out when grown.

12. *(b)* Frog's egg has a sticky gelatinous covering for protection, whereas, bird's egg has a protective hard shell.

13. *(d)* *X*–Birds and *Y*–Insects.

Birds have feathers which allows them to fly high and they have sharp beak which help them to eat.

Insects have wings which helps them to fly and stings which helps to them to take their food (blood) from host body.

14. *(b)* Birds have a 3-stage life cycle:

Egg → Young→ Adult. Whereas, insects have 4-stage life cycle:
Egg → Embryo → Larva → Adult

15. *(d)* Tadpole has gills to breathe while frog have both lungs and gills. Frog can live on land and water both and hence, called as amphibian. Tadpole has a tail while frog has no tail.

16. *(a)* Lizard, turtle, snake do not take care of their eggs to provide warmth to the eggs. Whereas, hen, sparrow and ducks sits on their eggs to provide warmth to them.

17. *(a)* Reproduction is the process to produce one's own kind. Hatching is breaking of egg shell by chick to come out. Moulting is repeated shedding of skin by larva to become an adult.

18.
(b) Eggs of butterfly have hard shell which protects them.

Butterflies have four stages of life cycle.

Egg → Embryo → Larva → Adult

Frog's eggs have gelatinous covering and no hard shell.

19.
(b)

	Parent		Young ones
A.	Cockroach	(iii)	Nymph
B.	Butterfly	(iv)	Cocoon
C.	Frog	(i)	Tadpole
D.	Bird	(ii)	Chick

20.
(c) They are blackish skin colour. This quality is not their adaptation. Black colour absorb more heat. Their adaptations are:
  (i) They can stores water in its hump.
  (ii) They have long eyelashes and transparent eyelid to get rid of sand of the desert.
  (iii) The have thick lips.

21.
(d) A bird having beak but no teeth, does not help in flying. Flying is done by the use of wings, feathers and body weight. Beak is not a characteristic need for flying.

22.
(b) All mammals have hairs on their body. *Platypus* lays eggs but they have all other features of mammals from which having hairs on body is the one.

23.
(b) Dog eats both plant products and animal meat, so its an omnivore. Leech sucks blood from the host animal, so is called parasite. Elephant eats grass and is called herbivore. Lion eats other animals and thus called as carnivore.

24.
(d) Tortoise has a hard shell that protects them from its enemies. Monarch butterfly has poisonous substances to protect itself.

25.
(a) Butterfly lay eggs on leaves of plants. Eggs then grow into larva, a caterpillar-like stage. This then enters into pupa stage which grows into adult butterfly.

26.
(d) Birds migrate from one place to other in reach of food. They also migrate when there is a low temperature, to the moderate temperature. Some birds migrate to lay their eggs. The environment given to eggs help in the proper growth and development.

27.
(c) Collection of frog's egg is called as spawn. They grow into embryo which develops into fish like tadpole. Tadpole develops into an adult frog.

28. **Down**
  1. Group of owls is called as parliament.
(a)
  2. Arctic tern makes the longest migration.
(b)
Across
  3. Proboscis is the long mouth part of butterfly to
(c) suck nectar from flowers.

  4. Adaptation is the ability of living things to
(a) adjust or adapt to their surroundings.

  5. Dolphins are friendly sea creatures.
(d)
  6. Tadpole of frog eat tiny plants called algae in
(a) their surroundings.

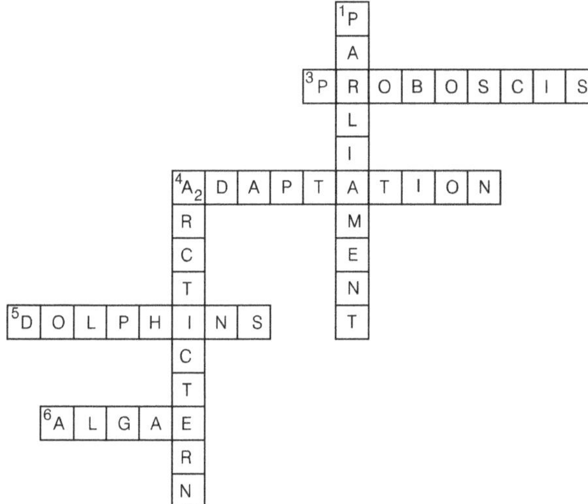

29.
(c) A tailor bird makes its nest by sowing two leaves together. It uses its beak as a needle. The nest is lined with wool, dried grass and cotton to keep it warm.

30.
(d) The Siberian crane comes to India to breed in winter. It can be seen at Bharatpur Bird Sanctuary in Rajasthan.

⒊ Plants

1.
(a) Life is not possible without plants on Earth. Plants are the only producers of Earth. They gives us food to eat and air to breathe. If there will be no plant, then all organisms will die and no life will be possible on Earth.

2.
(d) A plant can utilise its prepared food in its growth and in repairing, its damaged parts. Rest of the food is stored in them which animals and humans consumes.

3.
(a) When we are testing starch in the leaves, we first boil the leaf in water so as to soften it. Then we boil it in alcohol by keeping the beaker containing alcohol in boiling water. This decolourises the leaf.

Now, we put iodine solution over it. Its turning blue-black shows the presence of starch.

4.
(b) Alcohol could catch fire, as it is flammable, so it should never be heated directly over flame.

5.
(a) Boiling in alcohol is done to remove chlorophyll from the leaf so that the colour does not interfere with the result of the test.

6.
(c) Iodine turns starch blue-black, so it confirms the presence of starch.

7.
(a) So that leaves will not be able to make food during this time due to the absence of sunlight and will utilise all the stored food. Hence, when we'll test plant will recently prepared food .

8.
(c) Black paper does not allow the light to pass through the leaf. When sunlight does not pass through it, the plant will not able to do photosynthesis. And hence, leaf does not turn blue-black on addition of starch solution.

9.
(a) Stomata are present on the surface of the leaves and they help in exchange of gases and transpiration.

10.
(c) *Cactus* plant have leaves in the form of thorns, but they are green and waxy. These both conditions allows them to do photosynthesis and they prepares own food.

11.
(b) Crotons also contain chlorophyll but the green colour is not visible due to the dark red colour of the leaves. So, they also perform photosynthesis.

12.
(a) Plants are classified into two categories terrestrial and aquatic plants.

The plants which grows on land are called terrestrial plants and the plants which grows in water are called aquatic plants.

13.
(a) Aquatic plants may be free-floating, underwater plants, fixed water plants and emergent plants. Terrestrial plants may be coniferous trees, mangrove trees, desert plants. Deciduous trees and evergreen trees.

14.
(b) Plants need sunlight for their survival and for the preparation of food. Beyond 20 m depth, the sunlight cannot be reached. Hence, it is not possible to survive in a environment where there is no sunlight.

15.
(b) Roots of carrot absorbs mineral and water from the soil. It is a special kind of roots called as modified roots. These roots stores food within themselves.

16.
(b) Hollow leaves of pitcher plant are filled with nectar. When insects come to drink this nectar, lid closes and they are eaten by the plant.

17.
(a) Coniferous trees have cones and not flowers. Mangrove trees grow near water bodies so they have aerial roots to respire. Evergreen trees remain evergreen throughout the year. Deciduous trees shed their leaves in winter season.

18.
(a) Root system consists of roots. Shoot system consists of stem, leaves and flowers.

19.
(b) Carrot, radish, turnip and beat root store food for the plant and are known as storage roots.

20.
(d) Trees like banyan tree have roots which grow downwards from branches to the soil and are known as aerial roots.

21.
(c) Desert plants are not colourless. They do perform photosynthesis but not by their leaves. Their leaves are reduced to prevent loss of water. Their green stems perform photosynthesis.

22.
(b) A– Shoot system, B– Root system

Shoot system lies above the ground. The upper part is exposed to sunlight. Leaves helps in photosynthesis.

Root system lies below the ground. The lower part helps in the absorption of minerals and water.

23. *P—Flower; Q—Leaves; R—Stem; S—Roots*
(d)

24. *A— Fibrous roots B— Tap roots*
(b)

Fibrous root is a cluster of thin fibre like roots at the base of the stem is called fibrous root. These roots spreads out in the soil, e.g. maize, grass.

Tap root is the main root from which many branching roots grows sideways, e.g. pea, radish.

25. *A* is an orchid which take food and water from
(a) the stem of the tree to grow.

26. Such plants are called as parasitic plants.
(d)

27. Bud appears first and develops into a flower.
(a) Bud is the early stage of flower. After the development, it forms a flower.

28. *X—Petal (coloured part of flower);*
(b) *Y—Sepal (green leafy structure holding the flower)*

29. Across
(a)

1. Insectivorous plants grow in soil which is poor in minerals and so they eat insects for nutrition.

2. Stomata are the tiny openings in the leaf
(c) between cells.

Down

3. Paper was first made by people of egypt from a
(d) grass called *Papyrus*.

4. Flowers of a plant contains nectar which
(a) honeybees suck.

5. Corpse flower smell like a rotten fish.
(c)

6. Apiaries are the farms or place where bees are
(a) kept to obtain honey.

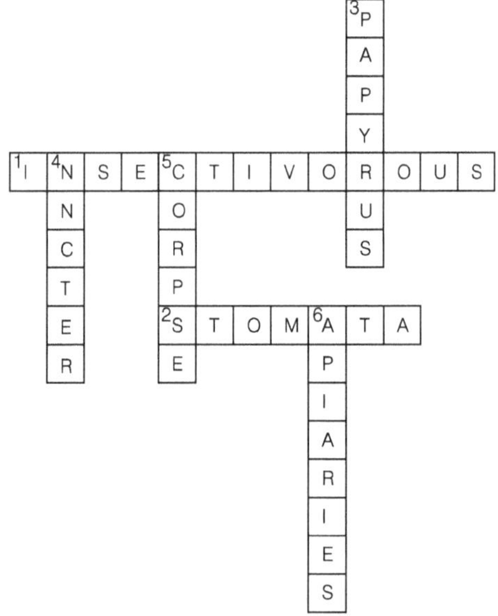

30. Photosynthesis is a process which prepare food
(c) using. Sunlight, water, chlorophyll and carbon dioxide.
Venation is arrangement of veins on a leaf. Chlorophyll is green pigment present in the leaves.

④ **Livings, Transportation and Communication**

Topic A – Livings

1. Figure 1 represents an apartment which is a
(c) pucca house. A house made of bricks, cement and iron is called a pucca house. Figure II is a hut, figure III is a tent house and figure IV is a houseboat.

2. People living in earthquake prove areas prefer
(c) to live in wooden houses with sloped roof. This type of houses help in saving their life. It is not harmful as wood is lighter than bricks.

3. Igloo is a white house made up of snow. People
(c) living in snow covered areas prefer to live in igloos.

4. *A – Wall*
(c)
B – Door

C – Ceiling

D – Window

5. Option (d) describes the type of room shown in
(d) first column most appropriately.

6. I. An igloo can be found is snow covered areas
(b)   only.

    II. Stilt houses are built above the ground. They
       are made up of wooden material. They are
       used as protection against flooding.

    IV. Tents and stilt houses are temporary houses.

7. People prefer to live in **societies** just like us,
(b) animals and **plants** also have their **habitats**. A
habitat is a special **place** where a plant or
animal **lives**.

8. Cloth cannot be used for making a house. A
(d) house is a place which protect use from rain,
wind, bad weather and thieves. Cloth does not
able to stop the rain.

9. Houses are mainly made up of strong and
(c) durable materials to reduce their cost of
maintenance and repair.

Topic B – **Transportation**

10. Metro trains run on special tracks hence, are a
(b) form of railways. It is a type of train only.

11. The roads which join the major cities of a
(b) country are known as national highways. Grand
trunk road is a name given to one of a national
highway which was originally constructed by
Sher Shah Suri.

12. Railways consume less time as compared to
(c) roadways, but more time as compared to
airways.

13. A. Airways   (iii) Helicopter
(b) B. Railways   (iv) Metro train
    C. Waterways (ii) Ship
    D. Roadways   (i) Autorickshaw

14. I. Highways are the ways which is a mode of
(a)   roadway. These are big roads and connect one
       city from other.

    II. Waterways is the cheapest mode of transport.

    III. Trains run on specially made tracks laid down
       along fields.

    IV. Bullock carts runs of tyres with no engine and
       no CNG.

    V. Roadways and railways are land transport.

15. **Boats** are one of the oldest type of **transport**.
(d) People use to travel through rivers and seas to
trade their goods in other parts of the world. In
many parts of the country, animals like **bullock**,

elephant and camel are also being used as a
means of transportation.

16. Tonga is a two-wheeled carriage drawn by a
(c) single horse. It is a common mode of transport
in the small towns of North India.

17. Camel carts are used in the desert. Bullock carts
(b) are used to carry vegetables and fruits in town
markets. Yaks and Ponies are used to carry
people and goods in the mountains.
Elephants were earlier used in the battle field.

Topic C – **Communication**

18. Except train, all others are means of
(d) communication. Means of communication are
the modes with which communication is
possible.
Television, radio and telephone is used for the
communication process.

19. Radio is a source of mass communication. Mass
(b) communication is a mode of communication in
which one can easily communicate with mass
that is a message can easily gives to a large
number of people.
Whereas mobile phone, radio and letter is a
mean of personal communication.

20. Newspaper and Magazines are print media. This
(c) is a mode of communication which is used to
communicate with large number of people. In
this media, the news and thoughts get printed
and exposed to large peoples.

21. Money order is a way of transferring money
(b) only. Postcard is a type of letter and takes long
time to be received. Parcel is used to send some
goods to a person. Speed post is the most
appropriate way to send an urgent message.

22. E-mail is the fastest and cheapest mode of
(c) communication for Faiz. E-mail is an electronic
mail which makes the use of internet. In e-mail,
one can easily attach pics and the sending of a
message only takes 1-2 seconds.

23.
(d) A. E-mail   (vi) Electronic mail
    B. FAX   (i) Facsimile Automated
                      Xerox
    C. www   (viii) World Wide Web
    D. AIR   (iii) All India Radio

24. **Mass** communication plays a crucial role in
(d) creating **awareness** among the people. It can deliver a **message** to a mass at a time. **Newspapers** and **television** are some examples of mass communication.

25.
(b)
  I. If a person needs to make a call to another person living in other city, then the call is STD—Subscriber Trunk Dialing, not ISD because ISD is made between two countries.
  II. ISD calls are made between two countries.
  III. STD stands for Subscriber Trunk Dialing.
  IV. STD calls are not made between two countries, they are made between two cities.
  V. Telegram is not the fastest means of communication. It takes one or two days to deliver the message. There are other modes which take only one or two second to deliver the message such as telephone, e-mail and FAX.

26. Transferring views and ideas from one person to
(c) another person is known as communication.

27. E-mail is a means of personal communication.
(c) It is not a mass communication. In e-mails, one person can communicate with other person only.

Telephone is a personal communication.

Newspaper is a mass communication.

Television is a mass communication.

28. Radio is a mean of mass communication.
(c) Whenever government need to announce any news or create awareness, it uses radio as a mean for communicator.

While e-mail is personal communication. Fax is not a interactive communication. It's a paper page type communication.

29. Animals were used for transport in ancient
(c) times. They were used to carry loads and for moving from one place to other.

30. Pests are a part of our homes. They get
(c) multiplied easily and becomes host in our homes. The chemicals which are used to bill these pests are called pesticides.

5 Our Body

1. Normal human heart beats at a regular rate which
(a) determines healthy working of the heart. Normal heartbeat or pulse of a healthy person is 72 times in a minute.

2. Epiglottis prevents entry of food into wind pipe.
(a) Food pipe and wind pipe lie parallel, but due to a flap like structure called epiglottis, food does not enters into the wind pipe.

3. Blood vessels carry blood from heart to body
(c) parts and also carry blood from body parts to heart.

4. 12 pair of ribs are present in the rib cage that
(a) protects our delicate organs like heart and lungs.

5. A– Lungs; B– Stomach; C– Heart; D– Brain
(c)

6.
(c)
  I. is false as our heart beats non-stop throughout our life.
  II. is true.
  III. is false as blood carries oxygen from heart to all body parts.
  IV. is false as digestion is the process in which complex food is changed into simpler food so that we can utilise nutrients of the food.

7. Air which we inhale through our nose also has
(c) many dust particles along with oxygen. Entering of these dust particles may cause blockage of respiration system. Small hairs in the nose prevents dust particles getting into the respiratory tract.

8. Nose → Pharynx → Lungs. Air enters through
(c) our nose then enters into pharynx and then enters into lungs.

9. All the activities which our body perform is
(d) controlled by our brain whether it is running, walking, talking, movement or any other activity.

10. Digestion is the process of getting nutrients
(c) and energy from the food.

Excretion is removal of waste from the body. Circulation is flow of blood to different body parts and heart.

Respiration is taking in oxygen and giving out carbon dioxide.

11. Digestive system is made up of many organs
(a) that work together for proper digestion of food. But large intestine is such a part of

digestive tract where no digestion takes place rather over here absorption of water occurs so that undigested food is removed out from the body.

12. *(a)* P: Kidneys; Q: Ureters; R: Urinary bladder; S: Urethra

13. *(a)* P, i.e. Kidneys filter our blood from wastes. It removes toxic substances.

14. *(a)* Kidneys are located below rib cage. In the rib cage, organs like lungs and heart are located.

15. *(a)* Kidneys and ureters are two in number, i.e. they are present in pairs. Whereas, urethra and urinary bladder are only one.

16. *(a)* Carbon dioxide which we breathe out comes from blood and the oxygen which take in goes into our blood.

17. *(c)* Lungs are those body parts into which oxygen enters and which only releases.

18. *(c)* Kidneys clean our blood.
Dengue is caused by mosquito biting.
Food must be covered.
Immune system is defence system of body.

19. *(a)* II. Kidneys filter and clear blood from wastes.
III. Water along with waste in form of urine move to ureter.
V. Ureters carry urine from kidneys to urinary bladder.
I. Urinary bladder temporarily stores urine.
IV. Urine is passed out of body by urethra.

20. *(c)* 'A' is the part which is the centre for intelligence. 'B' is the part which controls movement of the body. 'C' is the area which connects brain to spinal cord.

21. *(c)* A– Pharynx; B– Trachea; C– Bronchi; D– Lungs.

22. *(c)* A. Excretory system made up of kidneys, ureters, urinary bladder and urethra.
B. Circulatory system which consists of heart and blood vessels.
C. Digestive system which consists of stomach, liver, pancreas, small intestine and large intestine.
D. Respiratory system which consists of pharynx, trachea, lungs and bronchi.

23. Across

1. Urethra releases urine outside the body.
(a)

2. Antibodies of immune system are like weapons of an army. They fight with the enemies of the body, i.e. germs.
(a)

4. Larynx is responsible for production of sound. It is also known as voice box.
(c)

5. In stomach, food gets mixed with gastric juices that comes from stomach.
(a)

6. Fingerprints were used as signature in ancient Babylon in second millennium BCE.
(d)

Down

3. In lungs, the exchange of gases takes place. Oxygen gets in and carbon dioxide gets out.
(b)

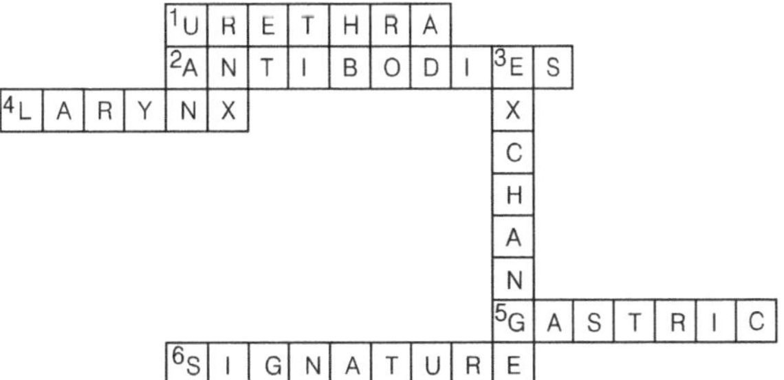

24. *(b)* Catching involves the use of hands.
Eating involves the use of tongue.
Walking involves the use of legs (foots).
Crying involves the use of eyes.

25. *(a)* Braille script is used by the people who cannot see. This is a boon for the people who cannot see. Now, these people can read and learn.

26. *(a)* Legs is not a sense organ. The organs which helps us to feel and sense the things around us are called sense organs. The five sense organs are eyes, nose, tongue, ears and skin.

27. *(c)* 206 bones are present in a human body.

28. *(c)* The tongue helps us to speak.

29. *(a)* Crutches are used by those people who does not able to walk. Leg is the body part for which it is used.

30. *(b)* Children suffering from polio learn to walk with the support of **callipers**.

(6) Food

1. Rice is a cereal, mustard is an oilseed,
(c) cardamom is a spice and black gram comes under pulses.

2. First the field is ploughed. Then seeds are sown.
(a) Fields are irrigated. Then the crops are harvested. Then threshing is done to separate grains from crops. Then winnowing is done to separate husk from grains.

3. Harvesting is cutting and collection of crops.
(d) Ploughing is turning up of soil before sowing seeds. Threshing is separation of grains from plants. Winnowing is separation of grains from husk.

4. Ist grains are cleaned, then packed and at last
(c) are labelled before they are sent to market for sale.

5. Farmers grow the crops, sell them and send it
(b) by truck driver to the worker in mandi. Then from mandi, grocer buys the grains to sell. From grocer we buy those grains.

6. 'P' senses bitter taste. 'Q' senses sour taste.
(c) 'R' senses sweet taste and 'S' senses salty taste.

7. Tongue senses taste due to the taste buds on
(a) tongue have nerves that tell the brain about taste of food.

8. All the given statements are correct. Tongue
(b) helps us to detect the taste of the food. It helps us to push chewed food into food pipe and also helps us to speak clearly.

9. Tiny bumps on the surface of tongue are called
(c) taste buds. With their help we can taste different food items.

10. Proteins are the body-building foods as they
(c) helps in building body and muscles. Vitamins and minerals are the protective food as they keeps our body fit and helps fighting diseases. Fats and carbohydrates are the energy-giving food as they provide us with energy.

11. Vitamin-A keeps eyes and skin healthy.
(b) Vitamin-B is good for muscles and nerves. Vitamin-C makes gums strong and heals wounds faster.

Vitamin-D makes teeth and bones strong.

12. Our two-third (about 67%) of body is made up
(a) of water. So, 95% is wrong. All other statements are correct.

13. Green leafy vegetables and milk and milk
(a) products both are protective foods. These foods makes our body healthy and helps it to work. Potatoes are energy giving food. They give energy to do work.

While pulses are body-building food. They helps the body to grow and repair.

14. Wheat, rice, cereal, bread are examples of food
(b) rich in carbohydrates. So, level-1 is rich in carbohydrates.

15. Level-3 food products are rich in proteins.
(c) Proteins help our body to build and repair different parts and cells.

16. Level-1 food is rich in carbohydrates.
(a) Level-2 food is rich in vitamins and minerals.
Level-3 food is rich in proteins.
Level-4 food is rich in fats.

17. Carbohydrates provide us with quick energy so,
(a) they are to be taken, i.e. level-1.

18. This person is overweight and this condition is
(a) termed as obesity.

19. The stall has an open environment. It easily
(b) catches flies, dust and germs. The food items and easily exposed to dust and flies.

20. Different steps of digestion of food are, after it
(a) is churned in mouth by teeth....
  I. Churned food from mouth enters oesophagus.
  II. Food enters stomach where mashed food changes into semi-solid form.
  III. Liquid food moves to small intestine.
  IV. Digested food passes then wall of small intestine to blood.
  V. Liver, gall-bladder and pancreas help small intestine to complete digest of food.
  VI. Undigested food and water enters large intestine and finally passes out through anus.

21. A– Mouth; B– Oesophagus; C– Liver;
(d) D– Stomach; E– Small intestine. This is called as digestive system.

22. In large intestine, undigested food is stored.
(b)

23. For proper digestion of food we must take care of few things like; we should have food at fixed hours of time. We should eat balanced food. We should eat slowly and chew food well. We should not overeat.

24. *(d)* Milk can be preserved by boiling, meat can be preserved by freezing. Peas can be preserved by dehydration and pickles can be preserved by salting.

25. Across

1. *(b)* Tea and coffee are common beverages. Leaves of these plants are used to make drinks.

2. *(a)* Digestion is the process of breaking down of food into simpler substances so, that it can be used by the body.

Down

3. *(a)* Thin layer of food gets deposited on teeth and gradually becomes yellow. This layer is called plaque.

4. *(c)* Undigested food passes from large intestine into the rectum. From there it passed out as faeces from anus.

5. *(a)* Langar is served in Gurudwara. This service of free food was started by Guru Nanak dev ji.

6. *(d)* A shark can have up to 3000 teeth.

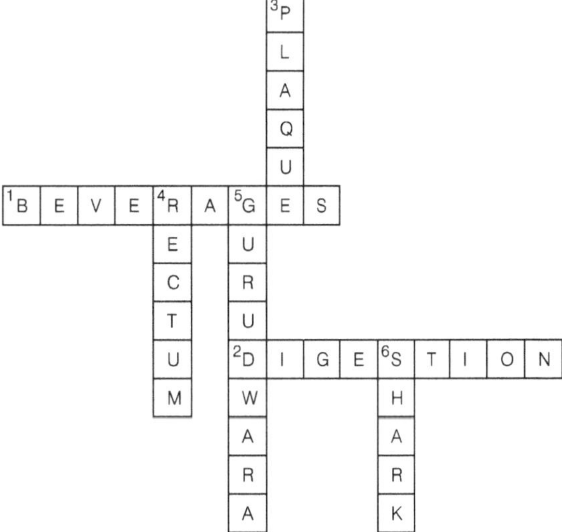

(7) Our Universe

1. *(d)* Galaxy contains stars and solar system. Solar system contains Sun, eight planets, their Moons and other celestial bodies.

So, option (d) is correct in context with the increasing order of their size.

2. *(b)* Moon is a non-luminous object whereas, stars are luminous but very far away from the Earth. When the bright sunlight strikes Earth, it makes it impossible for light from other stars to be distinguished and hence, we do not see stars and Moon during daytime.

3. *(b)* Earth is blue and green in colour because of the presence of water and trees on its surface.

4. *(d)* Venus is the hottest planet because of its cloudy surface. It is also known as evening and morning star because it can be spot in sky during evening or morning time as a bright star.

5. *(b)* Earth orbits around the Sun in West to East direction due to which Sun appears to rise in East and sets in West direction.

6. *(c)* Stars are millions of kilometers away from the Earth surface. More the distance between them and Earth surface, lesser will be their brightness.

7. *(b)* The correct statement for I is Earth takes 24 hours to rotate on its own axis once. The process is called as rotation.

8. *(d)* Rotation of Earth upon its axis causes some part of Earth lightened by sunlight thereby causing variation in day and night.

9. *(b)* During a solar eclipse, Moon comes between Sun and Earth and shadow of Moon falls on Earth. Also, we have to consider the size of all the three bodies. Sun is largest among them and Moon is the smallest.

10. *(d)* Rotation of Earth on its own axis is the cause of occurrence of day and night. As the Earth rotates, a part of it experiences day. The part which is not facing the Sun experiences night. Rotation of Earth occurs on its axis, not around the Moon.

Revolution The Earth revolves around the Sun in a fixed and elliptical orbit. It takes one year or 365 1/4 days to complete one revolution. Revolution causes the seasons on the Earth.

11. Uranus is the only planet that rotates sideways
(c) all other statements are correct.

12. Option (d) is correct.
(d) As constellation is a group of stars named for some recognisable figures which was seen by astronomers in ancient times.

13. The celestial body 9 which is orbiting around
(b) the Sun is Pluto. It is now considered as dwarf planet.

14. 2 is Venus and 5 is Jupiter. There are 2-planets
(c) between Venus and Jupiter. These are 3-Earth and 4-Mars.

15. The correct sequence is
(d) Mercury, Venus, Earth, Mars, Jupiter, Saturn, Uranus, Neptune.

16. Motion of Earth around the Sun cause variation
(d) in seasons. They are caused due to the revolution and the axial tilt of the Earth.

17. I. Solar system does not contain milky way
(c) galaxy. Galaxies are present in the universe, not in the solar system.
II. Venus is the hottest planet of solar system.
III. Pluto is not included in the solar system. It is called as dwarf planet.
IV. Moon is the natural satellite of a planet.
V. Group of stars which make some recognisable shape is known as constellation.

18. Our **universe** consists of many objects which
(b) include Moon, stars, planets and many more. All these objects are known as **celestial** objects. They all revolve around the Sun in predefined **path**. Celestial objects can be luminous like **stars** and non-luminous like **planets**.

19. I. During the new Moon day, Moon is not visible.
(a) II. **Crescent** Moon is the small portion of Moon that appears after new Moon.
III. Complete Moon is visible on **full** Moon day.
IV. Surface of Moon is not smooth, it contains many **craters** of different size.
V. Moon is **non-luminous** object. It does not have light of its own.

20.
(c)

A.	Shooting star	(iv)	Meteors
B.	Morning star	(vi)	Venus
C.	Blue planet	(vii)	Earth
D.	Red planet	(v)	Mars
E.	Natural satellite	(ii)	Moon

21. Our solar system contains eight planets and
(d) their Moons.
There is only one star in our solar system.

22. Our solar system exists in outer spiral of Milky
(b) way galaxy.

23. Moons are the natural satellites which orbit
(b) around the planets.

24. Across

1. Place where astronauts live and work in space
(c) —Space station

3. Planet which is surrounded by bright rings
(a) —Saturn

5. A person who travels in space —Astronaut
(d)

Down

2. Our solar system consists of planets—Eight
(b)

4. All the planets revolve around this star in our
(c) solar system—Sun.

6. This planet is also known as morning or evening
(a) star—Venus.

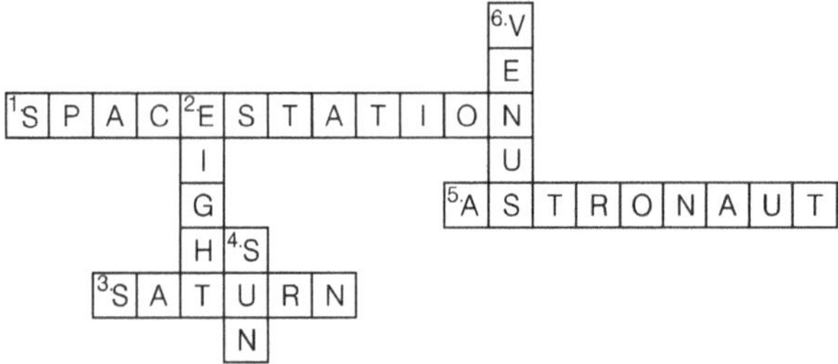

25. Axis of the Earth is an imaginary line that
(c) passes straight from North pole to the South pole.

26. Japan is known as the land of the rising Sun,
(c) because it is the first country to experience sunrise. This is because it is located at the extreme East of the Eastern hemisphere.

8 Water

1. *(a)* Sewage water is first of all filtered to remove immiscible impurities and the process is called filtration. Hence, option (a) is the correct answer.

2. *(c)* Chlorination is a method of water purification in chlorine gas. Chlorine tablets are used to clean water and make it free from germs. Hence, option (c) is the correct answer.

3. *(c)* Adding sugar to water makes a solution and is not used to purify water. Hence, option (c) is the correct answer other statements are correct.

4. *(c)* Both building canals and rainwater harvesting is to prevent uneven distribution of water in a country. Hence, option (c) is the correct answer.

5. *(c)* Water vapours present in air when come in contact with the cold surface of glass cools down and condenses like tiny water droplets all around the surface of glass. Hence, option (c) is the correct answer.

6. *(a)* Since, the water is initially boiled and beaker is closed by the lid so, the water vapours condense to form tiny water droplets in the inner portion of lid. When kept in freezer it turns into ice which is a solid state whose shape will not change when tilted. Hence, option (a) is the correct answer.

7. *(c)* Boiling water for 15-20 minutes kills all the germs and make water fit for drinking. Filtration method cannot separate germs from water. Hence, option (c) is the correct answer.

8. *(b)* Sand can be removed using filtration and sugar can be separated using evaporation. Hence, option (b) is the correct answer.

9. *(d)* Rainwater harvesting, purification of sewage water and using water judiciously. All the three options are correct in conserving water.

Rainwater harvesting is a technique which is used to conserve rainwater using specially build houses. That water can be used for washing, cleaning and for other purposes two.

Purifying sewage water by chlorination and other techniques are highly beneficial. It is a recycle process.

10. *(d)* A dam is used for many purposes like building canals and reservoirs, generating electricity and to prevent flood. Hence, option (d) is the correct answer.

11. *(d)* The correct labelling should be

A–Evaporation is a process in which water from the lakes, rivers evaporates and turns into water vapour.

B–Condensation is a process in which clouds in form of water vapours condenses to given water droplets.

C–Precipitations is a process by which the clouds converts into that cloud which is ready to give shower of water droplets.

12. *(c)* Sun provides heat energy which increases the rate of evaporation of water. Hence, option (c) is the correct answer.

13. *(b)* Pesticides used in farming, bathing of livestock, car-washing, sewage waste from houses and factory wastes being disposed in a river causes water pollution. Hence, option (b) is the correct answer.

14. *(c)* The water pollution makes water unfit for fishes and other aquatic animals making their life in danger. Hence, option (c) is the correct answer.

15. *(c)* Block C is partly sinking and partly floating. Same is the case with block A. Hence, option (c) is the correct answer.

16. *(d)* The above experiment only depicts the variation in shape and having definite volume of water and does not specify mass concept. Hence, option (d) is the correct answer.

17. *(c)* Water can occupy the space between marbles. So, option (c) is the correct answer.

18. *(c)* Clouds are the solid form of rain. Hence, option (c) is the correct answer.

19. *(b)* Reservoirs are the artificial fresh water bodies build at the back of a dam.

20. *(d)* As the cup is invertly lowered, air inside the cup escapes out of the hole and water fills the cup remaining the overall level to be same. Hence, option (d) is the correct answer.

21. Apart from sewage disposal there are many
(b) other causes of water pollution like industrial waste, oil spill, etc. Sewage water can be reused and make fit for domestic purposes. Hence, option (b) is the correct answer.

22. Seawater can be made fit for drinking by the
(c) process of evaporation and condensation of water vapours. Hence, option (c) is the correct answer.

23. Water is an essential component to sustain **life**
(b) on Earth. Earth is covered with **70%** of water. But out of this, only **1%** of water is fresh. The fresh water bodies include **lakes**, rivers and ponds. Sea and oceans include **salty** water.

24.
(b)
   I. During **precipitation**, clouds convert into rain drops.
  II. **Water cycle** involves circulation of water from oceans to clouds.
 III. Use of fertilisers and chemical pesticides which gets washed into rivers causes **water** pollution.
 IV. Water which is suitable for drinking is known as **potable** water.
  V. The rain water which seeks into the ground and collected there is known as **rain cycle**.

25.
(c)
   I. The level of underground water in an area is known as ground water.
  II. Water vapours falls as snow when the atmosphere is extremely cold.
 III. Water does not condenses when heated. On heating, water evaporates.
 IV. Fresh water is a new renewable resource. We can only clean it and reuse it.

26.
(c)

A.	Large water area surrounded by land	(iv)	Lake
B.	Hand pumps	(vi)	Ground water
C.	Farmers depend unit to irrigate their fields in India	(v)	Rain
D.	It covers the largest proportion on Earth, but not fit to drink.	(ii)	Ocean
E.	A channel taken out from a river or reservoir	(iii)	Canal

27. Precipitation of clouds causes rain. Hence,
(c) option (c) is the correct answer.

28. Rainwater percolates in the ground and
(b) increases the ground water table. Hence, option (b) is the correct answer.

29. Across

 1. Drinking water is also known as – Potable
(b) water.

 3. This waterbody is used to extract salt by the
(a) process of evaporation – Oceans.

 6. An artificial lake being made at the back of a
(a) dam by collecting river water – Reservoir.

Down

 2. The unwanted material that makes water unfit
(c) for drinking – Pollutants.

 4. This fresh water body originates from glaciers
(d) or springs – Rivers.

 5. The process of converting water into water
(b) vapours – Evaporation.

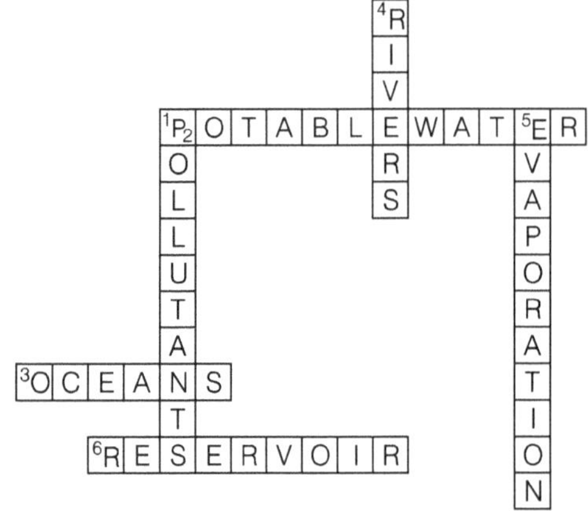

9 Work, Force and Energy

1. A pulley is a simple machine which consists of a
(d) grooved wheel and a rope. It is used to lift things easily.

Lever is also a simple machine but it does not consists of wheel and a rope. It is used to lift weights. Scissors and bottle openers are example of levers.

Inclined plane is simply a slope over which a load can be pushed up or down. A plank of wood is often used to load heavy barrels onto trucks.

Wheel and axle is a simple machine. It is made up of two circular objects of different sizes. The wheel is the larger object. It rotates around the smaller circular object called axle.

2. Wheel and axle is a simple machine which uses
(b) a wheel with a rod joined through its centre. Inclined plane is simply a slope over which a load can be pushed up or down. Screw looks like a nail with grooves cut into it. It is used to hold things together.

3. A staircase is a type of inclined plane which can
(b) be used by a person going to second floor. Eating a sandwich is not a simple machine. Running across a ground is not a simple machine counting money is not a simple machine.

4. Inclined plane is a simple machine which uses a
(d) slanted surface connected from a lower level to a higher level used to carry load through a height.

Wedge is a type of knife with edges are sharp in front and blunt at the back. They are shaped like two inclined planes attached back to back. It is used to cut hard objects.

Screw looks like a nail with grooves cut into it.

Lever is used to lift weights, cut things and open lids.

5. A fork is a wedge which consists of two inclined
(a) planes joining back to back. Using a wedge, the inclined planes are pushed into the object to tear them apart.

6. An iron girder can be easily lift using pulley.
(c) Lever can be used to hold pieces of plastic

together. To cut food, knife can be used which is a form of wedge.

7. Height is not considered as a force. Friction
(d) weight and gravity are a form of force. Force is defined as a push or pull of something. Friction is a force which help is stopping the object, weight exert force and gravity is a force which is due to the magnetic field of the Earth.

8. All the examples discussed are form of pulley. A
(d) pulley is made from a wheel and a rope. It is used to left things easily.

9. In case of a loudspeaker, the electrical energy
(b) supplied gets converted into sound energy.

10. The figure depicts class 1 lever in which
(b) A is load, B is fulcrum and C is effort.

11. Scissor is not a form of wheel and axle. It is a
(c) lever. Scissor is a simple machine which is used to cut things.

Car steering wheel and door knob are examples of wheel and axle. This simple machines are made up of two circular objects of different sizes. The wheel is the larger object. It rotates around the smaller circular object called axle.

12. Inclined plane is the simple machine which is
(c) used by the Geeta. An inclined plane is a simply a slope over which load can be pushed up or down.

Wedge is not used by Geeta because a wedge is a simple machine as like of knife whose edges are sharp in front and blunt at the back.

Stair case is a type of inclined plane.

13. The force of gravity on Earth is six-times
(a) greater than Moon because of which the block kept on Earth surface will weigh six-times heavier than the one kept on Moon.

14. Option (c) is a wedge. Wedge is a simple
(c) machine which is like a knife whose edges are sharp in front and blunt at the back.

Option (a) and (b) is a see-saw which a lever. It is used to lift the objects.

Option (d) is a scissor used to cut things. It make the work easy.

15. Hammer is a lever whereas a screw driver and
(c) door knob both are wheel and axle type of simple machines.

16. The diagram shows a class 1 lever. Scissor is a
(a) class 1 lever. Broom is a class 2 lever. Staircase is an inclined plane and a screw is also an inclined plane.

17. In a pulley system as the number of wheels are
(b) attached lesser will be the effort applied which means in case of two wheel pulley, the effort applied will be halved in the direction of gravity.

18. A claw ended hammer is a class 1 lever which is
(a) used to pull apart a nail from the wall. A wedge such as claw ended hammer is used to push a nail in the wall or in an object.

A lever such as screw driver is used to put the screw in the wall or in hard object.

19. In case I, the force applied does not displace the
(d) wall, so, no work is done. In case II, box is carried in hands, so, displacement will again be zero. In case III, book is stationary, i.e. at rest no work is done.

20. Screw is the simple machine which is used in a
(c) bottle cap shown below screw look like a nail with grooves cut into it. It is used to hold things together.

21. During the riding of a bicycle, mechanical energy
(d) is converted into kinetic energy. The mechanical energy of the boy is converted into kinetic energy which allows the bicycle to ride.

22. **Screw** is also a simple machine. It is basically an
(b) **inclined** plane wrapped around a **wedge**. This wrapped inclined plane is known as thread **narrower** the width of thread be **less** force will be required and less time will be taken.

23.   I. The ability to do work is known as **energy.**
(b)   II. A pulley consists of **wheel** and **rope.**
    III. Work is done when **force** applied on an object moves the object through some distance.
    IV. Anything which makes work easier is called **machine.**

    V. **Muscular** force is applied to make a machine work.

24.   I. The purpose of a simple machine is to make
(b)   work easier by allowing for a push or pull to occur over an increased distance.
    II. The bottom of light bulb is a screw.
    III. A compound machine is two or more simple machines that are working together to make work easier. They combine together to make work simpler.
    IV. A see-saw on play ground is a lever which is used to lift the objects.
    V. A pulley opposes the direction of applied force thereby making work easier.

25. The mass of the body is the amount of matter
(b) contained in it. A force when applied on a object, it can change the shape and the direction of an moving object but the mass of the object remains the same.

26. A– Image is a wedge. It is a like a knife which has
(d)   edges with sharp in front and blunt of the back.
    B– Image is an inclined plane which is simply a slope.
    C– Image is a lever which is used to lift the objects.
    D– Image is a wheel and axle which has two circular orbits.

27. Since, applying force on a wall does not
(c) displace it. So, no work is done.

28. If a force moves an object or changes the
(d) direction of motion of an object, then work is done.

Power is the rate of doing work. Gravity is a type of force which is due to the magnetic field of Earth.

29. When an object is at rest or does not move,
(d) then there are balanced forces acting on the object.

We cannot say that no force is acting on it, as the net force is zero. No stretching force is acting on it.

30. **Across**

(b) 2. When you push or pull, something you are applying– Force.

(c) 4. A scissor consists of two joined together– Levers.

(b) 6. Knife is a wedge, which used for cutting vegetables.

Down

(d) 1. When force applied on an object makes the object move is done– Work.

(d) 3. Sail on a sailboat are raised using this simple machine– Pulley.

(b) 5. A slide is an example of– Inclined plane.

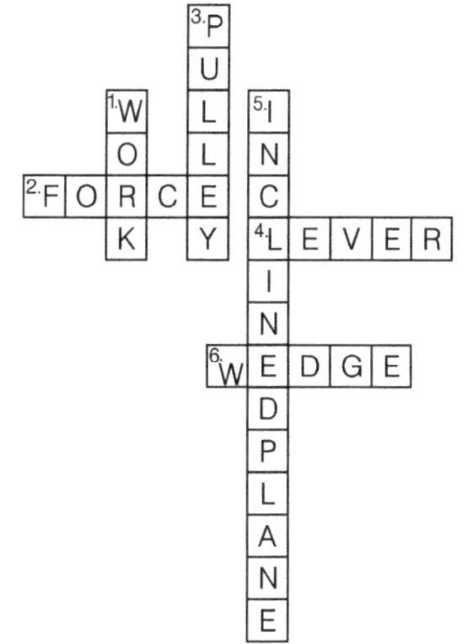

10 Our Environment

(a) **1.** We are more worried today about pollution because it is increasing day-by-day and affecting our lives. The increase in smoke, dust results in the birth of infectious diseases. We are now cautions about environment. Not because we care for the environment, but for our selfishness. Human is a selfish species. It only care for those things which is useful for them.

(c) **2.** If we use recycled waste water for cleaning purposes, then it does not cause water pollution. The water which we are using is recycled, the impurities are removed. Hence, can be used for cleaning purposes.

Releasing harmful gases into the air which will cause acid rain, putting unwanted waste in abandoned fields and throwing chemical waste products into rivers. All three cause water pollution.

(c) **3.** All the statements are correct. If we use biodegradable wastes and do composting to form manure, then that will increase the soil fertility.

More plants means they will bind soil and thus will prevent soil erosion.

Terrace farming reduces speed of the flowing rainwater and thus prevents soil erosion.

(a) **4.** The man is putting on the fire using wood which is basically a form of carbon when it is exposed to fire in the presence of air. The formation of carbon dioxide takes place which will increase in the concentration of carbon dioxide and results in decrease in the concentration of oxygen in the air.

So, option (b) is wrong.

It cannot release nitrogen as nitrogen is not present in free state (in oxide form). Nitrogen is usually unreactive also.

(b) **5.** There ears are affect by such a high volume and became deaf. The comfort level of sound for humans is 20-120 decibels. When human beings hear anything above 90 dB it becomes harmful for us.

(b) **6. Radioactive pollution** It is the pollution caused by radioactive or nuclear material such as uranium, radium, etc.

Water pollution is caused due to the addition of pollutants into a water body.

Air pollution is caused due to the release of harmful gases and particles in the air.

Noise pollution is the occurrence of load, disruptive and unbearable sound.

7. The change is because the pollutants are
(b) released by industries in the water. Hot water
and chemicals are dumped by the chemical
industries in the water bodies. These change are
not tolerate by the aquatic lives. They are killed
by these chemicals which causes the lake to
deplete.

8. Hot water and liquid chemical wastes are
(a) released by industry.

Rain water is the natural form of water. It
cannot be released by any industry.

Soap water cannot be released by industries. It
is used for further uses.

9. To save the lake or to stop it from further
(c) degradation, the industry should be warned to
first treat the wastes and then dispose off in the
water. This will reduce the concentration of
wastes in water which will keep the lake and
aquatic organisms healthy.

10. Soil supports life; both plants and animals :
(d) when chemicals such as dyes are leaked in the
soil, excess fertilisers are added to the soil
reduces soil fertility. Sometimes garbage which
not biodegradable is also dumped into the holes
of the soil which affects the soil fertility.

11. Soil pollution reduces the quality of the soil, soil
(a) becomes inefficient to support life and the soil
can even become poisonous due to the
pollutants. Pollution reduces the fertility of the
soil and thus fewer plants will grow on soil not
large number.

12. Burning of fuels, automobiles — Air pollution
(a) Landfills, mining — Soil pollution

Fertilisers, soil erosion — Water pollution

Other options are not corrected matched.

They are mismatched.

13. Carbon dioxide has the capacity to trap Sun's
(b) heat and not letting it escape out from the
atmosphere. It is released by automobile and
burning of fuels. So, it is the pollutant that is
responsible for such an increase of temperature.

14. The trapping of Sun's heat in the atmosphere is
(a) known as greenhouse effect and the increase in
temperature that this causes is known as global
warming.

Sun's trapping is not a natural phenomenon.
Earth's warming is the warming of Earth. When
the Sun's rays reach Earth, it gets reflects back
but due to smoke, dust the Sun ray's remains on
the Earth which results in warming of Earth.

No phenomenon is named as light house effect.

15. Pollutant's trap Sun's heat and does not allow it
(a) to escape. Due to the presence of pollutants
such as dust and smoke, the rays which comes
from Sun remains on the Earth. This results in
the warming of Earth.

16. Temperature of Earth rises → Rise in
(a) temperature causes melting ice of North and
South poles. → Lower and coastal areas may get
flood. → Loss of property and life and less land
for growing population to live.

17. Snowfall in Saudi Arabia, widespread floods in
(d) Europe, very heavy snowfall in Kashmir all are
the unexpected weather changes due to the rise
in pollution.

18. Ozone protects from harmful ultraviolet rays of
(c) the Sun.

Acid rain harms surfaces of buildings and soil.

Greenhouse effect causes rise in temperature of
Earth.

Pollution is contamination of the environment
with harmful substances.

19. Burning of fuel releases harmful gases → Gases
(a) remain in the air → Mixes with water vapours in
the air and come down with rain → Acid rain is
the result.

20.   I. We cannot control pollution is few days. Once
(d)   the pollution increases, this is very difficult to
    control the side effects of it.

  II. Factories should use filters that clean the air
    before released in atmosphere.

  III. CNG should be used in the vehicles.

  IV. Air pollutants like dust and dust particle may
    reduce vision.

21. **Biodegradable wastes** Vegetable peel, books,
(a) human excreta.

Biodegradable wastes are the wastes which
when mixed with the soil, is degraded by
bacteria. These wastes increases the soil
fertility.

Non-biodegradable wastes Plastic, glass, metals, thermocol.

Non-biodegradable wastes are the wastes which when mixed with the soil, is not degraded by bacteria. They remain in the soil and decreases the quality of soil.

22. Due to the pollution, surroundings look dirty
(d) and ugly. Diseases-like diarrhoea, dysentery, typhoid may spread due to the breeding of mosquitoes and flies. It also gives out foul smell. Therefore, all these statements are correct.

23. Burning is burning of garbage collected at one
(c) place.

Composting is when degradable waste dumped into a pit to convert into manure.

Landfills are in which garbage dumped in the open, away from a town or city.

In open dumping, garbage is dumped in the deep ditches which are dug in the ground.

24. 'Kabari wala' buy old newspapers and
(b) magazines from us to sell it to the factories which make fresh paper from the old ones by recycling process.

25. The 3R's to keep the environment clean are
(d) reuse, reduce and recycle.

The utensils, containers or polythenes which we obtain from the product which we consume, can be used for other purposes.

The use of polythene which is a non-biodegradable things should be in less quantity.

Paper and other biodegradable things can be recycled and used again.

Practice Set 1

1. Deer– pride are wrongly matched.
(d) Deer is a domestic animal. When animal are present in a group, then the group is known as herd, not a pride. The group of lion is known as pride. Lion is a wild animal.

All three options are correct.

The group of ants is known as colony.

The group of cows (domestic animal) is known as herd.

The group of owl is known as parliament.

26. Air is a mixture of gases that supports life on
(c) Earth. Nitrogen (78%), oxygen (21%) and other gases about 1%.

27. The Sun's heat which enters car by glass panes
(b) is not allowed to escape by carbon dioxide present in the car, thus increasing the temperature inside the car. Its almost similar to the greenhouses. This effect is called as greenhouse effect.

28. Down

1. By composting, we convert wastes into manure.
(d)
2. Excess use of fertilisers causes water pollution.
(c)
4. If we are making pencil holders from aluminium
(b) cans or plastic jars, we are reusing them.

Across

3. Ozone is thin layer of invisible gas in the upper
(a) atmosphere.

5. We should dispose off the garbage properly.
(b)
6. Air pollution can lead to reduced vision and also
(b) breathing difficulties.

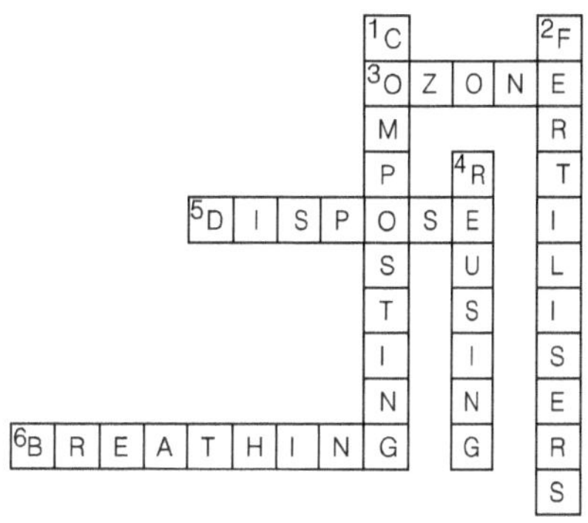

2. Cockroach has 3-stage cycle. Once, the eggs are
(a) laid, then after 6-7 weeks they are changed into nymph. Nymph is a adult cockroach which looks similar to cockroach, but does not has wings. Then, after many weeks of shedding their skin (moulting) nymph is converted to adult cockroach who has wings.

3. Toothache occurs as a result of some sequential
(a) steps which occur slowly in our mouth.

II. Bits of food sticks to the tooth.

III. Germs (bacteria) grow in the mouth.

IV. Germs breakdown the food particles which produces acid.

I. Acid creates cavity in teeth causing toothache.

4. Teeth break the food into smaller particles, so as to facilitate digestion process.
(a)

Saliva softens the food, so that it can be swallowed easily as its movement in the digestive system is smooth.

Tongue pushes bits of food to food pipe.

5. Absorption of water and minerals from the soil by roots. Roots are present in the soil. Soil have rich minerals and water. The function of roots is to absorb those minerals and transport it to the upper part of the plant.
(b)

The other options are not correct.

Release of water and minerals to the soil is not possible. If it does so, then plant will not able to survive.

Absorption of carbon dioxide from soil is not possible as soil only contains minerals, salts and water. Carbon dioxide is absorbed by the leaves from air.

Release of oxygen is not possible in root system.

6. X– Oxygen which is released by the plants into the atmosphere.
(b)

Oxygen is released by plant as a result of photosynthesis. Photosynthesis is a process by which plants prepare their own food.

Y– Carbon dioxide which is absorbed by the plants from the atmosphere.

To undergo the process of photosynthesis, plant need various assets such as sunlight, chlorophyll carbon dioxide and water. So, plants acquire the CO_2 (carbon dioxide) present in the atmosphere and completes its photosynthesis process.

So, carbon dioxide is represented by Y and oxygen is represented by X.

7. No, because it does not depend upon gravity.
(d) Weight of an object on Moon is 1/6th of the Earth is due to the difference in gravity of Earth and Moon. The relation between then varies is 1/6.

As we know mass is the total amount of matter in the body or object. The matter, i.e. the space occupied will remain same if the object will be on Moon or Earth, whereas the weight changes.

Weight is the force by which a body is pulled towards the surface. It is a force which a body exerts on a surface. So, it is a surface dependent phenomenon. That's why, weight varies with gravity and mass remains the same.

8. Earthworm lives under the ground. They are also called as 'former's best friend'. They makes the soil fertile.
(c)

Hippopotamus lives both on land and water. The animals which can live both on land and water are called as amphibians.

Horses lives in stable. The house in which horses live are called stable.

Woodpecker build their nests on trees and lives in them. Before Monsoon, they are able to built their nest in the bark of trees, which help them to survive in all the worse conditions.

9. I. In big cities and towns, people live in pucca houses. The pucca houses are made up of cement, bricks and iron pillars.
(c)

II. Kuchcha houses of villages need to be repaired as they are made up of mud, clay, husk and dried grasses, etc. The need time to time maintaince.

III. Dharavi in Mumbai is one of the largest slums in Asia.

IV. Multistoreyed building is a type of housing system in which multiple houses are built one over the other. This does not allow the water to get collected over an area. Mosquitoes generally breed over still water.

10. Leaves can be used to make manure. This is a method of 'Reuse' process. In this process, these dried leaves are buried under the soil through a pit. It gets biodegraded and helps in increasing the soil fertility.
(a)

All other three options are not correct. Burnt the leaves will create air pollution and increases carbon dioxide.

11. Satellites are used to know about the weather, to know the area of land and water. They are used for distant communication.
(b)

12. When we burn incense sticks in one corner of the house, we can smell it easily in all other corners of the house. This is due to the fact that gases flow easily and fill the entire space available. Gases have the property to acquire the entire volume. This property allows us to smell us the burning in incense sticks.
(a)

13. Number of milk teeth is 20 and number of
(a) permanent teeth is 32.

Milk teeth are those teeth which is acquired by child upto the age of 5 years. After that, it starts shading. As the age increases, new teeth comes in the mouth and reaches up 32.

14. Milk teeth are temporary and usually shaded.
(a) After that, new set of teeth are replaced called to permanent teeth. It remains in the mouth till the age of 30-35 years. After that, they will also fall. Then, no new set of teeth will come.

Option (b) is not correct. The falling of teeth does not depend on person to person (except when teeth are not brushed properly). Milk teeth has to be replaceable with permanent teeth.

There are only two types of teeth, e.g. milk teeth and permanent teeth. Deciduous teeth does not exist.

15. **Across**
1. Appearance of water droplets outside a glass of
(b) cold water is an example of condensation.

3. Melting is the process in which a solid turns into
(c) a liquid on heating.

4. Freezing is when a cup of water when placed in
(a) a colder region, turns into hard ice.

Down
2. Evaporation is the process of change of liquid
(a) into gas on heating.

Practice Set 2

1. Butterfly lay eggs under leaves of plants,
(b) whereas mosquitoes lay eggs on surface of water.

For the proper growth of any specie, special conditions are needed for the growth. For the egg of mosquitoe still water is a medium of growth. Water gives the food, temperature and safe environment for growth. For the egg of butterfly, water is not the correct medium. The egg is highly dependent on the food available in the plant, temperature and moist weather is the requirement for proper and healthy growth.

2. An adult frog can breathe through its **moist skin**
(c) in water and with its **lungs** on land. It has long hind legs that help it **hop** on land and **webbed** feet that help it to swim in water.

3. Incisors help you to bite the food. Canines help
(c) you to tear the food. Premolars help you to grind the food. Molars help you to crack the food. These are the four types of teeth. Molars are develop in the adult age of human being as a part of permanent teeth.

4. While eating carrot, we are consuming roots of
(c) the plants. These roots are modified roots. In this roots, the food is stored which is rich in vitamin-A.

While eating mango, we are consuming fruit of the plant. The fruit is rich in fibre and is very good for the good appetite.

While eating cabbage, we are consuming leaves of the plants. These are green leafy vegetables and act as a source of proteins. While eating sugarcane, we are eating stem of the plant. It is modified stem in which food gets stored. This is rich in carbohydrates and useful for the growth of the body.

5. A. (ii) B. (i) C. (iv) D. (iii)
(b) God has provided various organs to perform various functions.

A. Eating can be done with the help of mouth.
B. Counting can be done with the help of hand.
C. Reading can be done with the help of eyes.
D. Listening can be done with the help of ears.

6. Gravity of Moon is 1/6 than Earth. So, pull is also
(a) 1/6 of Earth. Therefore, a body will weigh 6 times less on Moon as on Earth. Therefore, if a body weighs 72kg on Earth, its weight will be 1/6 of it, i.e. 72/6 = 12kg.

7. Horses or horse carts were used by kings to pull
(c) their chariots.

Camels are used in deserts to carry goods and people.

Bullock carts are used to carry goods and people.

Yaks are used in mountains to carry goods and people.

8. These are eight plants. Series of planets as we
(c) move away from Sun is : mercury, Venus, Earth, Mars, Jupiter, Saturn, Uranus and Neptune.

So, A–Venus; B–Mars; C–Saturn; D–Neptune.

9. Rotation is movement of a planet around its
(a) central axis. Earth rotates once upon its axis in **24 hours,** whereas Neptune takes only **15 hours** to rotate once. Planet **Mars** takes same time to rotate once as the Earth.

10. To separate salt from water in a laboratory, first
(c) we need to prepare seawater, i.e. salt water in lab. So, the steps are like this,

IV. Dissolve 4 tablespoon of salt in a glass of water.

II. Pour this salt water into a pan.

I. Boil it until the water evaporates.

V. A layer of white powder forms at the bottom of the pan.

III. This white powder is actually salt.

11. Rainfed rivers are those which fill up by
(b) rainwater otherwise they have very little or no water. But Brahmaputra is not such a river. It has water all round the year.

So, this pairing is wrong.

Dam is a multistorage drainage system which is used to store water. This water is used for irrigation and also for the production of electricity.

Tubewell is a mode for the production of water in the rural areas. It is a form of ground water. River is a form of a natural water production. The rain water get stored in these rivers.

12. Water is a solvent as it dissolves many
(c) substances in it.

Sugar is a solute as it is to be dissolved in solvents like water or milk to form a solution.

Burning of candle is a chemical processes at it involves formation of new substance like carbon dioxide, etc.

Slicing of bread is a physical change as no change occurs in chemical nature of bread or knife after the action is performed,

13. Lungs and carbon dioxide are correctly paired
(d) as lungs are responsible for removing carbon dioxide from the body.

Kidney and body wastes are correctly paired as kidneys help body to get rid of body wastes.

Immune system and diseases are correctly paired as immune system can protect the body from diseases.

Brain is involved with thinking and not digestion. Rather stomach or intestines are involved with the process of digestion. So, this pairing is wrong.

14. Due to the chemicals given out by the factories
(a) near it. Factories near the Taj Mahal releases harmful chemicals which affect the whitening of marbles. These chemicals get deposited on white marbles and give it a yellowish colour.

Other three options are not correct marbles cannot became old as they are not living being. Marble is a chemical which is made up of calcium.

The visit of tourist is not the reason for yellow colour of Taj Mahal.